Bristol
VERMONT

Bristol
VERMONT

Historically Speaking

KERRY K. SKIFFINGTON

THE History PRESS

Published by The History Press
Charleston, SC 29403
www.historypress.net

Images are courtesy of the author unless otherwise stated.

First published 2009

Manufactured in the United States

ISBN 978.1.59629.666.4

Library of Congress Cataloging-in-Publication Data

Skiffington, Kerry K.
Bristol : historically speaking / Kerry K. Skiffington.
p. cm.
Includes bibliographical references.
ISBN 978-1-59629-666-4
1. Bristol (Vt.)--History. 2. Bristol (Vt.)--Social conditions. 3. Bristol (Vt.)--Biography. I. Title.
F59.B85S55 2009
974.3'5--dc22
2009023233

Notice: The information in this book is true and complete to the best of our knowledge. It is offered without guarantee on the part of the author or The History Press. The author and The History Press disclaim all liability in connection with the use of this book.

Contents

Contents

Preface

Taking Bristol Village as a whole its location, its beautiful Scenery, its desirable Soils for Roads, its water privileges, and its pure Mountain Air, all Combined, renders Bristol one of the most desirable locations in the State.

–Honorable Harvey Munsill, Esq.[1]

Like the early settlers of Bristol, I am "from away." In terms of credibility, that gives me both none and much. My children were born in Vermont and are being raised in Bristol, but are still from away and will always be so. It is part of the sense of long roots leading into the village.

Being from away has a lack of credibility, as reflected in the words of one member of the community upon hearing of my mission to write this book: "How long have you lived in Bristol?" Twenty years isn't very long in Bristol eyes and just shows the conceit of those of us who come to live here and somehow suck up the history as our own. You can't blame us. It's a beautiful history, of which those of us from away are often jealous. There are many families in Bristol whose names reflect those of the original settlers or of those who built its commercial base.

However, there is an interesting thing about small villages that gives outsiders some greater credibility: you will often see people from away sitting on select, zoning and development boards and other decision-making bodies. Locals sometimes rely on those from away to do some disagreeable or politically sensitive tasks or to be the ones to tread on delicate toes.[2]

As a recent example, it is primarily the people who have come to live here who make up the bulk of the community that is visibly opposed to the "gravel pit proposal" put forward by Jim Lathrop. It is not that true locals do not oppose it, but rather that the plan comes from one of the central businesses and older families of the community. Let the newcomers cross that Rubicon.

Being allowed into local governance has another aspect—it is a wonderful gift to those of us from other places because it also gives us permission to become locals someday. If we survive the criticism and the controversy (which is usually the case), we become part of the next generation's stories.

The other aspect of our credibility is that as people from other worlds we see with fresh eyes, leaving much of the received local wisdom aside because we simply do not know it. So when I tell a story that Sam McKinnon gave to the Folklife Center researcher, it's a new and wonderful revelation to me. It's not old news, and so I record it as fresh.

Will I probably fail someone in the village? Most assuredly. But will I add a new perspective that might just be interesting enough to local people, real locals and those from away? I think so. It is with that mission that I have undertaken the task of telling some of Bristol's stories in my own from away voice.

I was trained as a social anthropologist and taught to look at history as a living dynamic among people, not as a series of events reflecting important individuals (as history is often taught in schools). The Great Depression is less important to me, for example, than understanding how and why Gussie Levarn's mother sent food barrels to the daughter living in New York City, what was in them and the impact it made on the younger sister retelling the story as an old woman.

For those who are still living and/or about whom and whose families I am writing, I apologize for any misrepresentation or inadvertent blunder; the responsibility is my own. I have tried to record stories as I have heard them, passing no judgment, asserting no veracity and stating clearly, I hope, that this is "the way the story goes." This is a social, personal and story-based history. History is always written, they say, by the victors. In this case, the victors are those who consented to tell their own and others' stories as they understood them and to have them recorded and archived.

Acknowledgements

My thanks and gratitude go to the following people and organizations who helped me gather the materials needed to produce this book in the very short period of time of six months.

The content of the personal stories came primarily from tapes and transcripts provided by the Bristol Historical Society and the Vermont Folklife Center, and in personal communication.

Jim Cunningham got the word out early and provided photographs. The Old Farts Club (a self-named group of retired men), which meets every morning to discuss both old times and the troubles of the world, helped by answering questions and telling tales—probably "out of school"—but nonetheless willingly and knowing full well the purpose of my queries.

Nancy Wilson and the Lawrence Memorial Library provided the recording booth for people to tell their stories and for copious historic resources.

Thanks for the photographs go to Sylvia Coffin and the Bristol Historical Society, the former my guide through the latter. Also to the Henry Sheldon Museum, Cheri Rockwood, Jim Cunningham, Larry Gile, George Vince, Harland Wendel, Carol and Tom Wells, George Vince and Paul Bierman and Jamie Russell of the Landscape Change Project of the University of Vermont. With permissions granted by some of those mentioned, the project shared high-resolution versions of those photos free of charge.

Thanks also to novelist Chris Bohjalian and to Robin Vaughan for their advice.

I quote from *The Early History of Bristol, Vermont, Formerly Known as Pocock* by the Honorable Harvey Munsill, Esq., keeping his spelling, punctuation (or lack of it) and capitalization intact just as the Bristol Historical Society Book Committee did when it compiled the book from Munsill's papers and published it years ago.

I hope that those whose work is cited, whose stories are told (though I may not have spoken directly with them) and whose quotations have been used liberally throughout will feel that this book honors them and acknowledges their contributions. This is especially true for those living and deceased who consented to be interviewed, as well as those who conducted and archived them, so that our common history remains accessible. These wonderful interviews allow us to hear the stories in the participants' own voices and especially with their own insights, comments and senses of humor. Without them, this might have been just a boring old history book. I hope, instead, that it brings history to life.

Part I

Founding Families' Legacies

There are two Roads passing through the Village on East and West leading from New Haven to Lincoln and Starksboro; and the other leading from the South part of the Town to Monkton passing through the Village and crossing the first described Road nearly at Right Angle.

–Honorable Harvey Munsill, Esq.[3]

Bristol lies in Addison County with a population of 3,788 according to the 2000 census. The town in Munsill's time was then laid out just as it is today, with three main roads. From east to west, Routes 17 and 116 jointly pass through town as Main Street, where the downtown businesses are located. The other is called South Street and North Street, the divide occurring at Main Street and West Street at the corner of the town green, known until recently as "the Park." The third is below the Village—the north–south road where Route 116 comes through Bristol Flats and becomes Burpee Road, heading toward Monkton.

THE NEIGHBORHOODS

Bristol is made up of several neighborhoods, the names of which have been used since the early days, except for the name Bristol Leg.

Bristol Flats is the low-lying area south of the base of Stony Hill on either side of what is now Route 116, hugging the west side of the New Haven River. It was the first part of town to be heavily settled because of the fertility of its soil. Chartered in 1762, with permanent settlement beginning in 1786, there were fifty homes here by 1789. That was also the year that the name of the village changed from Pocock to Bristol. The first school and graveyard were built by that date, as was the first public house at Daniels Corners.

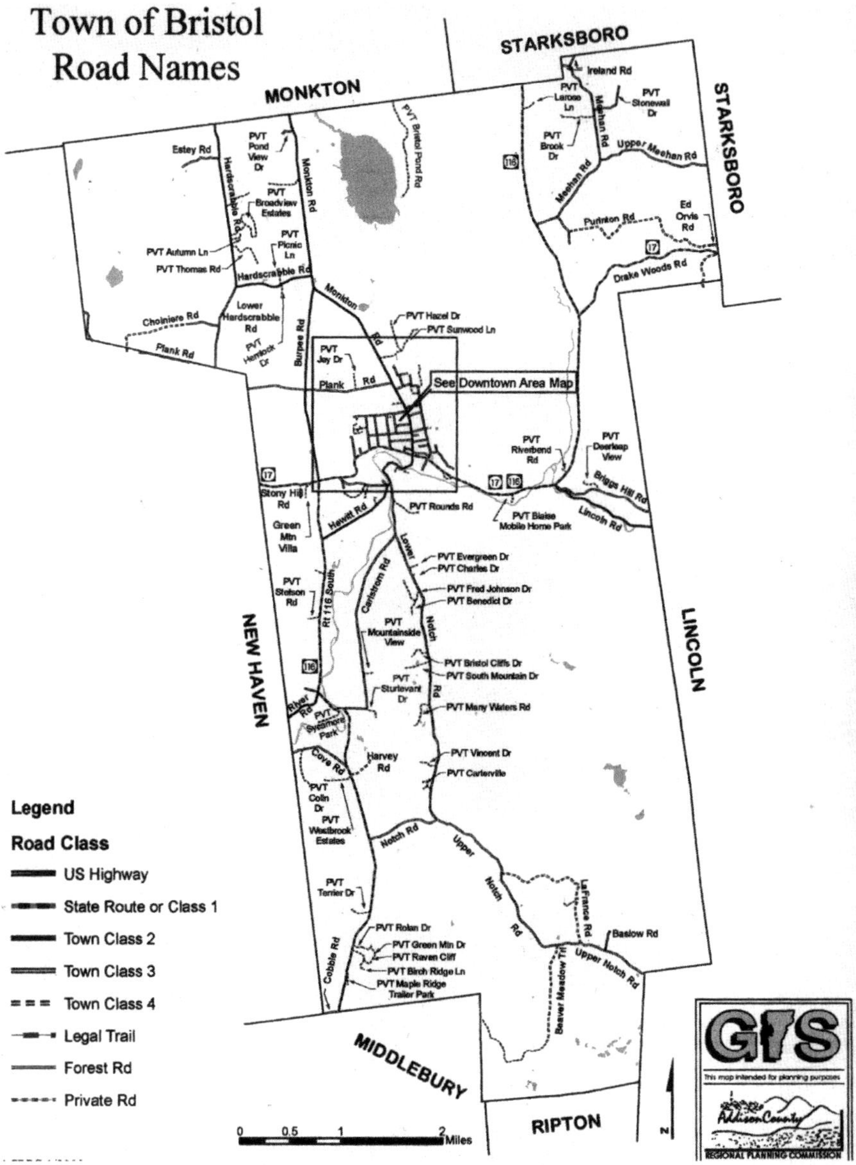

Map of the town of Bristol, 2009. *Courtesy of the Addison County Planning Commission.*

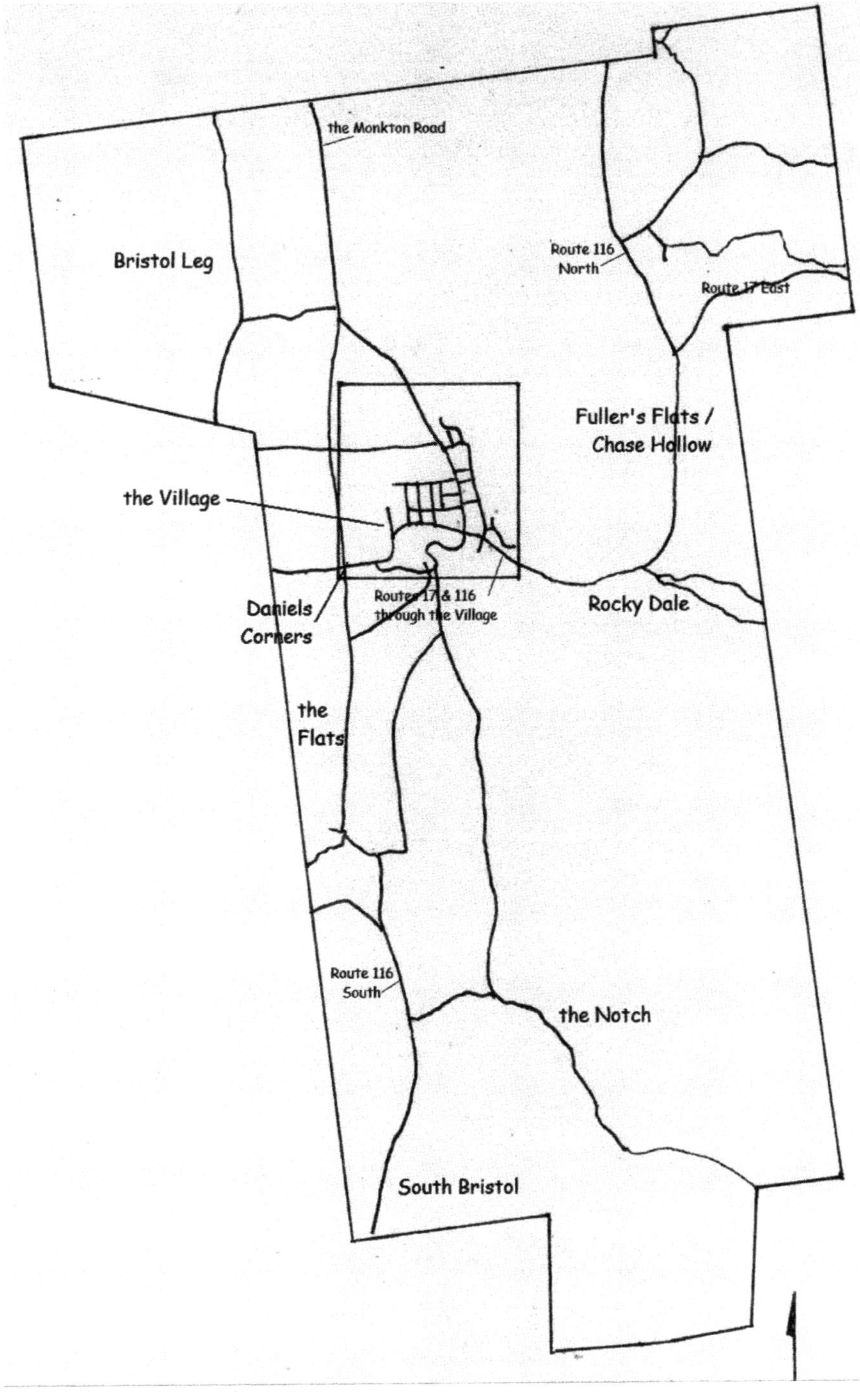

Outline of the town, showing neighborhoods and landmarks.

South Bristol lies farther south along Route 116 where River Road splits off, continuing south toward East Middlebury.

The Village is the central district surrounding the crossroads of North and South Streets with West and Main. It runs from the top of Stony Hill through the downtown shopping stretch, along East Street, toward Lincoln. It continues north on North Street until that road becomes the Monkton Road.

The Notch lies to the east of the Flats and south of the Village. This is hill, farm and forest. The Notch was also settled early and had one of the first schools.

Fuller's Flats is low-lying farmland that lies along Baldwin Creek and Route 116 north and east of town on the way to Starksboro. Chase Hollow, along the same stretch, is the ravine (named after Thurston Chase) through which Baldwin Creek runs as it enters Bristol.

Rocky Dale is located where the two bridges lie to the east, between the Village and Fuller's Flats. At this point, Route 116 turns northward toward Starksboro, and the New Haven River bends to the south along the road into Lincoln.

Bristol is laid out the same way now as then because, at base, our economy relies on the same things: the wood cut for lumber; the shops providing goods; the river, now more geared toward recreation as the new lifeblood of Vermont; and movement into and out of the mountains for milk, tourists, travelers and lumber.

ORIGINS

It is hard to imagine a place without a name or reason for existing from sometime in the past. Once a place is established, with a history and a well-known position in the economic sphere of something larger, in this case the state of Vermont, it becomes more difficult to see it as a clearing in the woods with a ne'er-do-well on the lam as its first white inhabitant. But that is what Harvey Munsill, the town's first historian, recorded in his papers:

> *Yet it is said and generally believed that there was a person by the name of John Broadt, a German* [or Dutchman by other accounts], *a fugitive from justice that made Bristol, then Pocock his place of residence for about twelve years, with no other company save that of his faithful dog and without seeing the face of any human being in said town, and supported himself by means of fishing and hunting and a few vegetables that he raised, and clothed himself with fur and skins.*[4]

By the time of this writing, there was "nothing remaining to mark the place where his rude habitation was located," though the author gleaned information that it was located "about one mile nearly south from Bristol Village and about 30 or 40 rods South Easterly from the Forge built by Munson, Dean & Gaige."[5]

This reflects the habit of local people to refer to places by their former use or ownership. This long-established Vermont custom leads the casual traveler or recent immigrant to believe that everyone in town knows everyone else. It has been argued, though, that it is just an artifice, a means by which newcomers actually learn of the interrelatedness of residents and also a quick way of teaching them local history.

One fact, however, should ease the mind of the beleaguered visitor or newcomer: no one in any of these villages or towns, Bristol included, really does know everyone. Instead, through the interaction of gossip, community activity and storytelling, locals know *of* one another. This is information accessible to everyone, at some level, if they pay attention.

So here was Bristol, even before it was Pocock, existing entirely as some fugitive's hovel. The story humbles us all: there are no descendants of this

An early frame house in Bristol Notch, one of the earliest parts of the town to be settled. *Courtesy of the Bristol Historical Society.*

John Broadt. So those who tell us their families have been here since the beginning are exaggerating.

"The first permanent settlement in Pocock…was commenced by Samuel Steward and Eden Johnson, who married Sisters."[6] These families came from Whitehall, New York. The Johnsons came by land, driving the cattle, and the Stewarts came by water up through Lake Champlain, landing at Vergennes. There they bought teams and headed through New Haven to Bristol. The families lived together until months later, when the Stewarts built a home farther west within the Village.

Elizabeth Abbott Stewart, the wife of Samuel Stewart, made unintended history of a sort, having survived the deaths of two infants and a serious illness before her arrival. One day when Samuel was away from home, a deer appeared near the house. Elizabeth took a gun and went outside, where the deer still stood, apparently unafraid. She used a log to steady her aim and fired, but the gun wouldn't fire despite several attempts. At this point, wrote Munsill, she "pecked the flint for the purposes of trying again" and did so—successfully. This, he concluded, "is believed to be the first deer killed in Bristol by any civilized person."[7]

Samuel and Elizabeth were the first white settlers in Pocock after Broadt. They came with the intention of permanently living in the town, and Samuel became one of the first selectmen. He had been a Revolutionary War hero, but it wasn't until 1786 that the family, along with Stewart's brother-in-law, Eden Johnson, began clearing land in Pocock.

The Stewarts had eight more children—two were twins, Harry and Harriett. They lost four: Harry within days of his birth and Elizabeth, Harriett and Electa to scarlet fever in 1803. The others presumably went with Samuel and Elizabeth when they moved west into Ohio in 1817, departing Bristol for good. The oldest, Chauncey, was born before the family came to Vermont and apparently joined the family in Ohio.

Apparently, all of the children and their families either went to the hometowns of spouses or to Ohio with the folks, but what if just one Stewart son had stayed? A Stewart did operate a gristmill on Mill Hill at the end of the 1800s, but he was of another family, unless one of this large brood quietly returned to Bristol.

Instead, with the rapid growth of the town, a whole new set of families had come to fill the roles of an expanding social and civic life and continue its history.

Bristol, though it was settled at the same time as many of the other towns in Addison County and elsewhere in the Champlain Valley, grew quite quickly. According to Munsill, "Its progress was steady so that in 1800 the number of its inhabitants was 734 and the Settlement commenced somewhat simultaneous in the different parts of the town."[8]

AMERICAN INDIANS

Truly native Vermonters, the American Indians were not yet gone from the community or fully absorbed within it soon after the first white settlement. The first marriage was that of Samuel Brooks and Betsy Rorapaugh, an Indian woman, on March 16, 1791.[9]

Even well into the nineteenth century, there was regular interaction between Bristol folks and Native Americans. When Nellie Martin's aunt, Catherine Casey, was a child in the 1870s, a group of natives, presumably Abenaki, "came down" and regularly held powwows on land owned by her father. This relationship was friendly, and locals would take food to the visitors. Nellie said that there was a cemetery up there that she tried to find some years later, but she believed that the cattle, which had since grazed in a pasture there, had probably buried the remnants of that cemetery beneath their hooves over the years.

Munsill himself described "relicks" left behind in Bristol by Native Americans, including some arrowheads found on his own property and on other farms and house lots in town. His chapter on "Aborigines" speaks highly of their skills and hardworking natures. "They are famed for great strength and activity, and capable of enduring great privations and hardships."

While Munsill noted the violence of some tribes, he also stated, "It is not supposed that any of these cruelties have been perpetuated…within the bounds of Bristol village."[10]

Munsill listed a great number of tools and other objects as proof that Bristol had been a sometime residence for native groups probably over a long period of time. In fact, he wrote of the same series of visits to Bristol during his lifetime as those witnessed by Catherine Casey:

> *Something more than a year ago an Indian burying ground was discovered a short distance North of the North line of Bristol in the Town of Monkton near the North end of Bristol Pond, and some four or five skeletons found in a sand bank.*
>
> *Something more than twenty years ago* [probably in the 1850s] *there were two or three families of Indians that came from the North and stopped a few weeks in the woods…*

> [A]*mong them was a verry old man who then called himself about ninety eight years of age, and who was quite intelligent and retained his memory verry well and could speake our language so as to make himself well understood, and while they were stopping there the writer…took an opportunity to…learn something of their history, habits and customs… The old man was suddenly taken verry sick, and soon died in his tent while stopping near Bristol village, and was buried in our burying ground at the foot of Stony Hill, so called. The Rev. Francis Whiting preached the funeral sermon and all the Indian in company with him, as well as a large congregation of our citizens, attended the funeral.*[11]

FAMILY NAMES OVER TIME

The stories that shape Bristol show that the family names among settlers were wound around one another in complex and interesting ways. It has long been the kind of town where families remain for generations. Many people come and go, but there is a thread of names repeated generation after generation. A wonderful reflection of the merging of families is seen in the names of married women before the late 1970s, when hyphenation became commonplace, as did the decision for a woman to keep her maiden name—Gertrude Hewitt Lathrop, Dorothy Purinton Trudo and Dorothy Lawrence Bosworth, for example. Even while their children and siblings leave the area each generation, those who remain continue as the social core of the town, their family stories also being those of the town.

In the first years of the town's organization, when records started being kept, Amos Eastman married Sally Hewitt, whose sister married Robert Holley. Robert Dunshee married Bershabee Eastman, and then the Munsill and Howden families were joined twice by the marriages of Gurdan Munsill to Betsy Howden and Henry C. Howden to Abigail Munsill. Early settlers Seth Peake and Robert Holley became related through the marriage of Peake's son and Robert's granddaughter. The only son of Harvey Munsill married a Holley—Charlotte M., daughter of John.

Many place names in Bristol are derived from these original families, too, or from others who farmed large tracts, built or owned downtown buildings or made contributions to the town. We have Brigg's Hill, the private lane of Drake Smith Road, the Hatch and Dunshee Blocks, Holley Hall and the Howden-Hall building. The Honorable Harvey Munsill's son Newcomb left the family name on Munsill Avenue. Later, other families gave their names to buildings such as Tomasi, the name emblazoned in granite above

Town of Bristol, Downtown Area

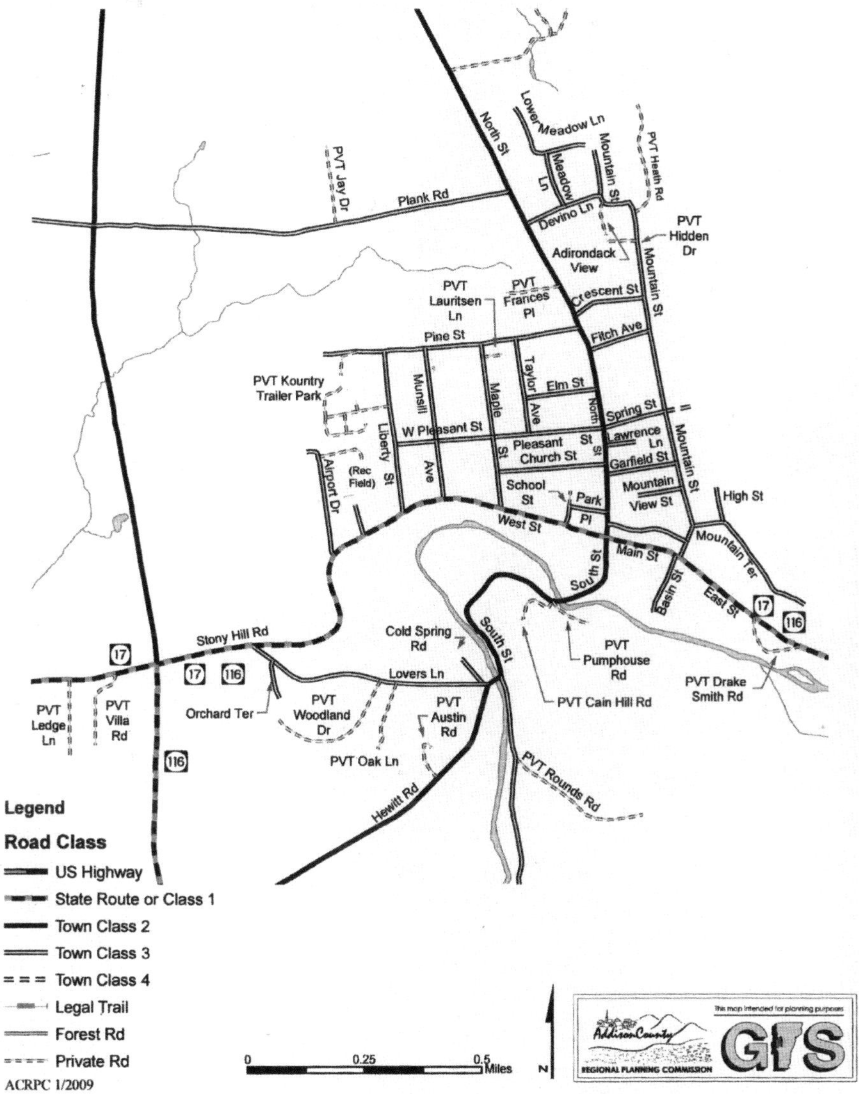

The town of Bristol, including the Village, 2009. *Courtesy of the Addison County Planning Commission.*

the second-story windows of the Tomasi Block on the north side of Main Street. Tomasis owned many businesses in the downtown area throughout the later twentieth century. The town's library bears the name of another, the Lawrence family.

The town has many houses that bear people's names, too: the Norton House, the old Lawrence place on East Street (which is not the Lawrence House on North Street), the Bosworth Homestead—home of the colorful sisters Helen and Grace and also to their nephew Dr. David M. Bosworth—and the Peake House, home of generations of that family.

The Bosworth family was a fixture in the town from 1868. Helen and Grace, the Reverend David's daughters, were famous in the town, not just because they lived in the large house on the corner of Park and North Streets or belonged to this important family. Grace was known as an artist, and a story is told with loving humor of Helen's fondness for using garlic in the winter months to ward off illness.

Four Hills Farm refers to the four members of the Hills family who now own and farm the land, which originally was called the Parmalee property and later the John Kilbourn land. The farm is also where Merritt Parmalee Allen, the writer known more for living in a home called the Maples, was born and raised.

The Thomas family has owned and operated businesses in Bristol for generations. At one time, members partnered in business with the Ridleys and the Drakes. One generation restored the Maples on Hewitt Road after it had fallen into deterioration. Today, it is one of the wonderful landmark homes in town.

Dan Thomas had a shoe repair shop on Main Street, Terry Thomas has been a builder and antiques dealer. His children, Adam, Aaron and Susan, own and operate Thomas Building and Design, Inc., which has recently renovated some of the oldest buildings in town.

The Hewitts, early owners of the Maples, gave their name to the road itself. Gertrude Hewitt Lathrop tells of her Hewitt ancestors' arrival in town. "Grandfather Hewitt (Elisha) came from Warren in 1887." She tells of his bringing a big safe with him by oxen and living in Bristol with six children, three girls and three boys. Her father, Harvey, married a South Bristol girl.

Her husband's family was descended from Noah Lathrop. She married his great-grandson, Earl Pearl Lathrop. Names are quite interesting in this branch of the Lathrops. He had been given the first name Earl, but there was some confusion over his parents' intentions over the middle name. "His mother sent his father to the town clerk," Gertrude explained. "She wanted him named after his father, Charles. He thought it was to be after her father,

The Ridley Parker Thomas family (early 1900s). *Courtesy of the Bristol Historical Society.*

Pearl. And he named him Earl Pearl." Gertrude's own family has many first names that begin with the letter *D*: twins David and Donald, Diane, Douglas, Dwayne and Dawn.

Earl managed his father's farm out on Bristol Flats at the colonial house sometimes called the Pillars because of the columns on its façade.[12]

The custom of carrying on in the family business and farming traditions continues today. One firm that sells fuel throughout the county is a true local family operation. The Jackmans have been delivering fuel since 1946, when Fred Jackman joined N.H. Munsill Hose Company, forerunner of the fire department, where he was chief for many years. He joined with his brother, Glenn, and father, Glenn Sr., operating Jackman's Coal and Coke Co., now Jackmans', Inc. The company had originally been purchased by Glenn Sr. and Clarence Lathrop from a coal distributor at the demise of the railroad. Fred married a Bosworth.

Alan Kilbourn considers himself related to everyone in Bristol. The Kilbourns ran the Cyclone Gristmill on Main Street. Alan's father's generation had five or six children, and Alan himself was one of five siblings who lived to adulthood. But he also counts as an ancestor Thomas S. Drake, of Drake, Smith & Company. As demonstrated by the Jackmans and the Kilbourns, the family trees of many local residents read like town histories.

OLD FAMILIES IN TOWN POLITICS

From 1792 through 1812, either Amos or Jonathan Eastman was town clerk except for two years (1808 and 1810) when James Day held that office. Both Amos and Jonathan were clerks during terms when they were not sitting on the select board. For those nineteen years, neither of these men was off the list of officers of the town.

Cypran Eastman (spelled elsewhere "Cyprian" or "Cyprain") was a selectman in the first four years of the town, while Oliver and/or Amos Eastman were selectmen for eight out of the same nineteen years (1792–1812) and more, sharing that office with Ezekiel Dunton, Daniel E. Parmalee, John Kilbourn (who seems to have held every office at one time), Isaac Drake and Gurdon Munsill. Robert Dunshee is listed as one of the very first three selectmen.

Robert Holley was representative for eight of those years, constable three of them and selectman once, showing up again a few years later in that role. Many of these men—for at the time, of course, only men could hold these offices—were also justices of the peace.

Later, John Howden, Noble Munson, Abraham Gaige, Solomon Drake and then Harvey Munsill himself held these offices for many terms, changing roles ever few years. The rolls of town officers in those early days read like a who's who of prominent and long-lasting Bristol names. Following them were their brothers, sons and/or grandsons: Winter Holley, Harvey Parmalee, Luman Munson, Datus Gaige, George Parmalee, Thomas S. Drake and more.

During those same years, some members of these families became college graduates in the professions, such as Anson H. Parmalee, Congregationalist minister, and Charles Smith. Other figures, not yet in positions of town prominence but to become influential men, were Royal W. Peake, Jeremiah Hatch and Erwin A. Hasseltine.

At the time of the writing of Munsill's papers, from approximately 1850 to 1870, those names were, not unexpectedly, repeated in the records of town meetings. For example, Munsill himself was moderator in 1865 and Datus Gaige in 1866; George Parmalee was town clerk during those years, with Luke Parmalee acting as selectman at the same time. Wolcott Howden was overseer of the poor, and Thomas S. Drake was constable. Other names listed during those town meetings were William Dunshee and Luman Munson as auditors and, as town treasurer, Horace Farr, a name only beginning to be heard in Bristol at the time.

Some of these early names, like Kilbourn and Parmalee, are still found aplenty in the population and others are now familiar as building names, like Dunshee, rather than in the grand list. Still other names, such as Soper, Grant and Dayfoot, disappear in the records altogether, with no Sopers or Dayfoots listed in the 2009 Addison County telephone books.

Part II

The Social Mix

There was none of the early settlers of Bristol men of large fortunes, but generally of very limited means requiring their constant labor with their own hands to subdue the forest, cultivate the soil as a means of subsistence for themselves and their families. A Log Cabin to afford them shelter for the time being was all that the most wealthy settlers could obtain.

–Honorable Harvey Munsill, Esq.[13]

The social mix within Bristol is rather the same as other towns in Addison County and elsewhere in Vermont. Those whose stories were recorded by Munsill were, in the main, the very visible settlers: visible as the first settlers and visible as merchants, landowners and early managers of the town's affairs. There were also those whose names and stories were more ordinary. It is also my aim to give those people faces. Among these are people of color and transients whose stories are largely told by others because they left no documents.

PEOPLE OF PROMINENCE

In May 1900, the largest taxpayers in the town were listed in the *Bristol News*. Among them were T.S. Drake, W.R. Peake, E.B. Patterson, Cornelia Smith, A.A. Dan's estate, Horace Farr's estate, E.C. Dike, C.P. Bush, E.S. Farr's estate and Noah Lathrop, the father of Bristol's lumber industry.

Other newspaper announcements described the careers of local notables like Erwin A. Hasseltine when he was elected probate judge in 1900. This kind of news brought potential economic prosperity because with it came the probate office itself. Alongside this announcement, Bristol was lauded as "the best business town in the district and the center for a large surrounding county."

These families also invested socially and financially—Cornelia Smith donated the land for Holley Hall; W.A. Lawrence was responsible for the building of the library; and the Munsons donated the parcel that became known as the Park, now called the town green.

The arrival of these families in Bristol is recorded in the previous histories of the town, county and state. For example, Robert Holley, who was born in Connecticut, migrated first to New York and later to Bristol. He held many offices within the town and represented us at the statehouse, even acting as state delegate to the 1828 Constitutional Convention. So within a brief time, these prominent families became intertwined in the social and financial fabric. They have been what might be called Bristol's social elite.

The Eastmans

The Eastman name is among those who first settled in Bristol when it was still Pocock. Jonathan Eastman came to Bristol with his brothers Calvin, Anson and Amos in 1791. Jonathan took an early role in the leadership of the growing settlement.

Ira, born in 1802, was the child of Jonathan and his second wife, whom he married in September 1792. A first wife bore him a daughter, Lydia, but her mother died before the brothers moved to Bristol. There were five children by his second wife, Ruth Dean. Ira married into the Foote family of New Haven. Ira's siblings were William D., Almon, Sarah and Jonathan.

The elder Jonathan died in 1816 at the age of sixty-three. His grandson was Albert Eastman, father of Frank L. Eastman, still living in Bristol in 1903 per a genealogical sketch.[14]

Jonathan's brother, Calvin, arrived in Bristol before his brother. Calvin lived sixty-six years on a single farm, the land he originally settled. This was unusual among those early settlers, who often bought and sold properties more often than twenty-first-century residents would imagine. Even Munsill noted the long tenure.[15] Calvin was also particularly long-lived, dying in 1856 at the age of ninety-five.

Oliver and Amos were the two youngest Eastman brothers, the seventh and eighth born in the family. Oliver had nine children. Unlike Calvin, Oliver moved from farmstead to farmstead, buying and selling properties.[16] Eventually, he moved his family out of town entirely, dying in New York State, but not before he, too, did service at various times as selectman and constable in Bristol.

Oliver's son, Cypran, Samuel Stewart, Gurdon Munsill and other early settlers were among those who eliminated rattlesnakes from their Bristol dens on the west side of South Mountain. It was the custom to hunt snakes early in the spring when they first came out of their nests. On one particular foray, the group claimed to have killed 180 snakes. At the time this was related, the writer noted that it seemed to be a very effective method of eradication, because at that time, 1940, it had already been one hundred years since rattlesnakes had last been seen in Bristol.[17]

Cypran died young but was also active in the affairs of the town; had he not died, he would likely have continued in this role as his uncle did.

The youngest brother, Amos, married Sally Hewitt of the Bristol Hewitts, with whom he had six children. He lived in and out of Bristol over many years, buying and selling real estate to residents Charles Lee Smith, Samuel Holley and John Howden, among others. He lived at times right in the Village, on North Street, at others out on Bristol Flats. When his first wife died, he left town again, remarried and returned. Nonetheless, he also held elected office. Like other men of his family, save Cypran, Amos died at a very advanced age.[18]

The Munsons

Noble Munson, another founding father of the town and holder of many offices over the years, resided first in Bristol Flats. He moved into the Village to set up a forge and lived on North Street.

His son, Luman Noble, one of six children, built the house on Park Place, opposite the green, where his parents also lived in their old age and where they died. The Park was donated by this family in 1827 "for the express purpose of a Public Common and Green."[19]

The elder Noble was the owner of the third Bristol forge, which he built along with Gurdon Munsill, Amos Eastman and Robert Holley. Its mechanical workings were said to be the best in Bristol at the time. Its end finally came in 1830—a flood on July 26 washed away so much that its precise location was nearly obliterated.

While the Eastmans' and Munsons' stories reveal the interconnectedness of these families and how some rose to become public figures in commerce or governance, the Drakes' story shows a thread of influence over time and through the generations.

The Drakes

Solomon Drake arrived in Bristol in 1805, becoming a landowner, business owner, a deacon of the Baptist church and frequent officeholder in town.

He married Cylinda Scott, daughter of Amos Scott. Of the couple's ten children, only seven survived to adulthood.

Along with farming, Solomon owned a gristmill and later the tanbark mill on the New Haven River west of the Lord's Prayer Rock. Upon his death, the tannery was taken over by his son-in-law, Horace Farr.[20]

Solomon's son, Thomas S. Drake, born on his father's farm in 1829, was also a successful businessman in Bristol. Not content with following a farming life, Thomas joined William Dunshee in establishing a general store or dry goods business, later a hardware store.

The 1903 biographical sketch of Thomas Drake records that "he had 'many irons in the fire,' being one of the busiest as well as one of the most enterprising citizens in the county."

Apparently so. At the time the genealogy was compiled, Drake was "manager, treasurer and secretary" of the electric light plant, dealing in real estate and building houses. It is widely known that he started what came to be called simply "the box company," Drake & Smith, which passed through many iterations.

Where A.J. Eastman had formerly built butter tubs, Drake and his partner, E.W. Smith, began in 1885 the manufacture of other kinds of wooden items: sleighs, wagons, boxes and cabinets for Victrolas. This building was the fourth of a cluster of buildings on the premises, including a sawmill and the tannery formerly willed to Horace Farr, which consolidated with the Drake & Smith Company. Somewhat later, the partners were joined by Charles McGee, who purchased several shares.

McGee partnered with the Farr brothers to build the Drake-Farr block on the south side of Main Street and, in 1898, became a president at the National Bank of Vergennes.

Drake married Sarah Ellen of New Haven, and three daughters were born. Ella, the eldest, later had two sons, Fred S. and Williard Mathison, who worked in their grandfather's box shop, now called Drake, Smith & Company.

Drake was long-lived; the 1903 account of Drake's life noted that "his career covers more than two-thirds of the nineteenth century…Mr. Drake was an observer of or participant in many of the most important events of his state and nation for more than two generations. He was born while Andrew Jackson was serving his first term as president. He was seventeen years old when the United States declared war against Mexico. He watched and waited the turn of events during the…Civil War."[21]

William A. Lawrence

W.A. Lawrence grew up in Monkton and came to Bristol in 1881 to leave farming behind. He went into business, speculating in horses and cattle, and was well known for this throughout the north country by 1900.

The house in which he lived on the east side of North Street at the base of Spring Street was built in 1897, and as a dealer in real estate, he had other homes built around the same time. Perhaps the Norton house, standing on the west side of North Street on the north side of Pleasant, was among them. The Queen Anne style of them is quite similar.[22]

Lawrence is the man whose name the library in Bristol bears, in memory of both of his wives, who were equally involved in library affairs.

The Holleys

Robert Holley was a native of Connecticut and a veteran of the Revolutionary War. He and his family arrived in Bristol in 1795, living first on Bristol Flats and later in the Village. Holley ran a mercantile shop there. He also held many offices in town and was a representative in the legislature and delegate to the Constitutional Convention of 1826.

As the father of eight children, he contributed in a wider way to the growth of the town. Samuel, later a judge and political force in town, and Winter Holley, a successful businessman, are among the best-known sons. A daughter, Samantha, married the doctor, Joseph Needham. Well-known grandchildren were Charlotte and Cornelia.

The Holley and Munsill families were tied with the marriage in 1851 of Charlotte Holley to Harvey C. Munsill, the judge and historian. Their elder son, Newcomb H., began what became the Bristol Fire Department (see part three). The couple had a daughter, Seraph, who died at the age of three, and another son, Charles.[23]

The Holleys also became linked to the Peake family when Samuel's daughter, Jane, married Royal Whitman Peake in 1831; their son was Willis Royal Peake.[24]

While the prominent or official citizens of the town have usually or often been men (because men had that prerogative more than women), several women contributed in their own right and not solely as wives, mothers or daughters. Among these is Cornelia Smith (née Holley).

Cornelia Smith's story is scattered in one or two lines in the histories so far written about Bristol. We know that she was the granddaughter of Robert Holley, one of the earliest settlers. She was the daughter of his fourth son,

The Lawrence House, on North Street, now the Crystal Palace Bed-and-Breakfast (2009).

Winter B. Holley. Apparently, she amassed considerable fortune, either through inheritance or her own abilities, as she is listed among major taxpayers in 1900.

Her most enduring and visible (and yet nearly invisible, since her own name is not attached to it) contribution to the town was in homage to her father. The land for the town hall was given by Cornelia Smith. It was not named, as commonly believed, for that original settler.

The Norton House stands kitty-corner to the Lawrence House. The house was remodeled extensively to keep up with the Lawrences (2009).

Holley Hall, named after Winter Holley by his daughter, Cornelia Smith; it was built in 1884. *Courtesy of Jim Cunningham.*

Holley Hall marks the "center" of Bristol and is the location for many of its activities, from town government and the voting polls to concerts, fundraisers and dances.

BRISTOL RESIDENTS FAMOUS IN THE WIDER WORLD

Of course, Bristolites have made recognized contributions in the wider world. Among these were Merritt Allen, Jeremiah Curtin and Florence Cragen.

Jeremiah Curtin, born in 1835, was well known as having been essential to negotiations with Russia during the Civil War, for that country's help was vital to the success of the Union cause. Curtin traveled a great deal, translated books and wrote his own. The inscription on his tombstone, written by President Theodore Roosevelt, notes that Curtin spoke seventy languages.

Merritt Allen, a native of the town, was another writer of note. Having suffered from polio at seventeen, Allen was confined to a wheelchair for most of his life. His choice of a writing career was shaped, at least in part, by the limitations imposed on him as a result. In the year of his death, 1954, an obituary lists his accomplishments of "more than twenty-eight books for boys," short stories, radio serials and plays and notes that he made contributions to numerous anthologies.[25]

He lived at the Maples with Vera Cline, his one-time nurse, and Gertrude Parmalee, the three of them having purchased the home together. He was said to use as his study the room originally built as a nursery.[26]

Florence Cragen took a different path than most of Bristol's women before the 1970s. Her motto was that "service is the rent for your room on earth." Consequently, she ran for election as representative to the legislature and served many years as one of the forty-six women in the legislature during the 1940s. The opportunity for women to become involved in statewide politics was made possible because so many men were serving in World War II.

Born on Maple Street, Cragen grew up with Helen and Grace Bosworth. Her father built houses on Garfield Street and along Mountain Street, and for nineteen years he was general foreman at Bristol Manufacturing.

As an adult, she owned and operated the Ben Franklin store with her husband, John. She joined the Outlook Club, eventually becoming its president. That experience, she later explained, was what gave her the skills and confidence to pursue her seat in the legislature. After she left the statehouse, she continued in politics and was appointed by the governor to be the first woman in the country to chair her state's board of social welfare.[27]

The Maples, or Hewitt Homestead, was built by Albert Dunshee in 1847 and bought by Elisha Hewitt in 1888. The couple here is unidentified (1880s). *Courtesy of the Bristol Historical Society.*

BAD BOYS AND BOSSES

Bootleggers smuggling liquor into Vermont from Canada were apparently not uncommon. Growing up as a child in Hinesburg, Gussie Levarn, longtime Bristol resident and storyteller, and her friends would identify any stranger or "bogeyman" character as a bootlegger, as stories of selling alcohol illegally during Prohibition were commonplace. The same was probably true in Bristol where her cousins lived.

There are no documents recording bootleggers and their activities in town and certainly no stories known to be factual. Nonetheless, Frank Brady, who lived on West Street, was rumored to bring contraband liquor into Bristol. It was also assumed that this was known by townspeople, some of whom must have been customers. It was said that Brady was seen to be particularly well off. Apparently, he went frequently to Montreal, and any place to which he brought liquor was also said to be in the business of prostitution (something that could be said of Brady directly, as well).

Dr. Deb Brown recalls tearing down a very large concrete chimney shortly after moving into 26 West Street in 1959, a house that had been built in 1889. When Dr. Brown bought the house, he was afraid that a serious crack in the chimney would bring the whole heavy thing down onto the house, so he had it removed. When it came down, he said, there were two large flues, both clean as a whistle and which had never been used. Given the rumors about Frank Brady, the state of the chimneys suggested where large amounts of smuggled liquor might have been stored. There were also bars on every window in the basement, for which Dr. Brown had no ready explanation.

Even in the upper social echelons, bad boys became legend. Gussie Levarn told of the crooked real estate dealer who sold farmland in the years after World War II. This man allegedly filled the wells with potable water when the well had, in fact, gone dry. At other times, he would gesture toward a meadow and comment on what good soil it had, implying that it was included in the sale when it was not, when the acreage was less than the unsuspecting buyer might believe. The buyers of these properties would only find out the truth after the papers were signed and they either found their well dry or began to plow the meadow, an angry neighbor at their door.

Employers were sometimes hard on their hired men and laborers. "Old Derwood," a farmer on Lower Plank Road, was such a man. He had a good farm and was himself reputed to be a good farmer, but it was also said that he "worked the hell out of his help." There is an exemplary story about the hired man who broke his arm in an accident. The self-absorbed farmer complained about the terrible timing of this event, because it showed how inconsiderate the hired man was, as haying time was just starting.

Juna Perlee told about other nameless farmers who were tight-fisted with their farmhands. One hired man worked for room and board and tobacco. The farmer agreed that he was the best hired hand the farmer ever had, but he had to let him go. He worked hard without complaint, but the farmer fired the man because he just used too much tobacco, costing the farmer "a fortune."

Another farmer's wife was concerned that their hired man was eating her out of house and home, especially consuming too much butter. So, as she served homemade, unsliced bread, she decided to cut the bread thicker so he would eat less bread and therefore less butter. But, having overheard the plot being hatched, the hired man picked up one of the largest slices and buttered both sides.[28]

ETHNIC GROUPS

Munsill's history illuminates the variety of ethnic origins represented by many Bristol folk. But other families with deep local roots were of French or Irish descent. Both groups came in search of new homes and more prosperous lives. African Americans and Native Americans have also called Bristol home.

Native peoples were respected by the people of Bristol, even if their customs were different. The stories suggest that the respect was mutual. Ethnic divide does not seem to ever have been a critical part of Bristol history, but there are two ethnic groups that, at the time of their arrival, sometimes suffered negative stereotyping, while others among them were important people of status. These were the Irish and the French Canadians.

Irish

An Irishman was one of the original Bristol residents. Henry McLaughlin came to America as a drummer boy for the British general John Burgoyne. He never went home but moved to Bristol in 1787, having married Mary Dunton of Dorset. Her brother, Ezekiel Dunton, already lived in the village and later became a general in the Bristol militia.

Henry McLaughlin, the original surveyor of Bristol's roads, was an important citizen in town, being on the committee to raise funds for roads and building bridges, as well as the setting out of lots of land for settlement. He also held public office. Besides his occupation as surveyor, he owned the first brick building in Bristol, a tavern at Daniels Four Corners, until 1800.

A bizarre twist of fate for this family's story explains why this is not among those names still heard in Bristol. Henry and his wife moved to New York but returned just once to Bristol to visit friends in 1813. Here they became victims of an epidemic of spotted fever, dying within days of each other. They left a son, Thadeus, who became the first postmaster in 1803, operating the post office from his father's brick building. However, he also moved to New York State and remained there.[29]

Many of the families in Bristol today are descendants of the neighborhood called Little Ireland in Starksboro. Gussie Levarn, for example, tells of Kevin Heffernan, who she believed was an officer in the Irish army before he came to the United States. When he died, an Irish organization, she said, took part in his funeral service in Bristol. Her husband, Rosie, "was a Meehan," descended from the Irish Meehan family who lived at one time in South Starksboro and gave their name to at least two roads.[30]

Some of those with Irish heritage probably came into Bristol directly, but the Little Ireland connection is central. Those Irish came at the time of the potato famine in Ireland in the 1850s, at least one family settling in Monkton first. Gerald Heffernan told the Bristol Historical Society that his own great-great-grandfather worked at the kaolin mine in Monkton. He contracted arthritic rheumatism on the job. It was only then, when his son was a twenty-year-old man himself, that that particular branch of the South Starksboro Butlers settled in Little Ireland.[31]

These Irish were not originally farmers, but they found themselves farming poor land in Starksboro. The men often came from working in the trades, as did Heffernan's ancestor. When they were unable to find work or became ill at their jobs, they changed occupations, becoming rock farmers.

French

Locals still talk of French neighbors. When describing the men living next door to her, Gussie referred to them, not unkindly, as Frenchmen[32]—meaning French Canadian. So many local names, like Trudo, Devino and Cousino, tell of the large numbers in Bristol's population who came from north of the border. They came at different times and for different reasons. That they were of French origin or spoke French was an important marker for others in town.

Alan Kilbourn tells of his own "French" mother, whose maiden name was Emma Brassard. Her family had come from the Granby area looking for fertile farmland, eventually settling in Bristol. She was married to John Kilbourn, owner of the Cyclone Gristmill.

As early as the 1770s, French families came down from Quebec and settled in the area north of the town center, between Lake Winona (Bristol Pond) and the village center. Often the incoming "French" were poorer than the Bristol children, and sometimes they came unable to read or write. Local children were known to sometimes target those children for ridicule and tricks, as bullies exist in every town in every era.

Still others came from more prominent backgrounds. For example, Charles L. McGee, born in Bristol in 1851, was of Canadian-born parents of French heritage. McGee became a foreman at Drake & Smith and later bought an interest in the firm. He became part owner and manager by 1903 at the age of forty-eight. It was he who, following his beekeeping hobby, brought to Drake, Smith & Company the idea and expertise to manufacture bee boxes.[33]

Joseph Julian Dumas was also of French descent, though more directly through his grandfather, who emigrated from there, first to Canada and then to Vermont. Dumas came to Bristol in 1859, working briefly as a

A French shopkeeper on Main Street; note the sign: "[J.?] Z. Gaudet, Harness Shop" (circa 1880). *Courtesy of the Bristol Historical Society.*

cabinetmaker. Later, he was among those fighting at Gettysburg, before returning to Bristol in 1876 to work at Bristol Manufacturing Company.[34]

African Americans

With Vermont being "the whitest state in the union," it is somewhat curious to find one of the town's liveliest stories to be about an African American resident. Arthur W. "Dude" Prince is mentioned elsewhere in this history (part six).

Photographs from the archives show at least one African American family living in a cabin in Bristol in the late 1800s, though who they were and what happened to them is not recorded.

In 1840, among a list of business owners is the name of Andrew Santee, described in parentheses as "colored."[35] He made his living as one of three blacksmiths in town. Of him and his family, nothing more is known.

We know that Vermont country towns have had African Americans living in them. Alexander Twilight attended Middlebury College and Rokeby in

An unknown African American family (1892). *Collection of the Henry Sheldon Museum, Middlebury, Vermont.*

An early one-room framed house; the people are unidentified African Americans (circa 1870). *Courtesy of the UVM Landscape Change Program and the Bristol Historical Society.*

Ferrisburgh was known to have been a stopping point for fleeing slaves on the Underground Railroad. Former slaves Daisy Turner (whose story is told in a children's book published by the Vermont Folklife Center) and poet Lucy Prince also lived in Addison County. It is a pity so few of their stories have been remembered.

Vanishing into history without a trace will not happen to Dude Prince, however, as his name has been added to the landscape. Prince Lane runs from Shaw's Supermarket to Mountain Street, below Phoenix Rising.

Gypsies

Gypsies may be the one group that had any clearly expressed prejudice attached to them. They arrived every summer, camped on open fields with the permission of landowners and remained for a time selling products that they made. Gussie Levarn told of gypsies who visited Hinesburg regularly in her youth. According to her, "They made baskets. And when they were selling baskets to my mother, there was someone else stealing something. You had to watch out for them."

They weren't necessarily feared, as they treated local children to pony rides at their camps, to which it seems they must have had permission to go. Children were fascinated and not afraid of them, as they were of bootleggers.[36] The gypsies were more unlike the locals, more unlike even than Indians or African Americans. They wore different clothes, it was true, but probably more importantly, they kept to themselves and didn't socialize with local people. The native groups that similarly came and went did, as we have seen, invite a social connection with the people of Bristol, creating relationships with them over the long term.

Part III

Structural Core: Building a Town

These are to warn the inhabitants of Pocock to meet at the dwelling house of Justin Allen, in said Pocock, on the first Monday of March next, at 10 o'clock A.M., to act as follows: 1st, to choose a moderator to govern said meeting; 2d, to choose a town clerk, 3d, to choose selectmen; 4th, to choose a town treasurer; 5th, to choose a constable; 6th, to do any other business thought proper to do on said day..

– Elijah Foot, J.P. New Haven, February 14, 1789,
quoted in H.P. Smith's History of Addison County, Vermont[37]

While the French were having their own Revolution, kick-started by their participation in ours, Pocock was born. The second town meeting was held at the home of Benjamin Griswold, and from then on within the Village but still at either the schoolhouse or in the private homes of Henry McLaughlin, John Ketcham, Noble Munson, Oliver Eastman and Robert Holley.[38]

The start of the construction of Bristol's public buildings seems to have been the forerunner of Holley Hall:

> *The first permanent place for town meetings was a room in the Bristol High School which was completed in 1856. In 1855, when plans were under way to construct the new High School, the Selectmen provided $600 toward the cost of the school in exchange for the privilege of a town meeting room in the building.*[39]

Later, in 1883, land was given for the building of the town hall (see part two). Holley Hall was completed in 1884 and continues to be the main meeting place in the village. The police department and town management are directed from the basement. Before the high school built its own facilities in 1930, this hall was used by the school for its public gatherings and as its

Constructing the bell tower of Holley Hall. William Holley, the son of settler Robert, once ran a dry goods store on this site (1900–1902). *Courtesy of the UVM Landscape Change Program and the Bristol Historical Society.*

gymnasium.[40] At one time, it had also housed a jail, which now provides storage space for town records.

Later, the other public building of note, the Lawrence Memorial Library, was built. The collection began in the coldest months of 1893 with the Bristol Library Association, financed by subscription of the members. By 1902, its collection of magazines plus 1,090 books was given to the town, establishing the Bristol Public Library.[41]

As with Holley Hall, it wasn't until a personal donation was made, in 1911, that the library manifested as a building. It was built as a memorial to Lawrence's two wives. His first wife was Lockie Partch, a teacher from Hinesburg, who died in December 1889, after having given birth to six children. In 1901, Lawrence married Minnie Peet, born Morrison but at that time the widow of Anson W. Peet, who was killed in 1906 in a Rutland Railroad collision. Gerald Heffernan's Aunt Lizzie was severely burned in the same accident, as no doubt were many others. Minnie had no children with Lawrence, and none of Lockie's children settled in Bristol, perhaps explaining why there are few Bristol Lawrences listed in the phone book in 2009.[42]

STREETS AND ROADS

Before the town was organized, the major roads as we still know them were surveyed by Henry McLaughlin, laid out and built to the standards of the day. These roads, set out by the proprietors to whom the original charter was given, were in place when the first meeting of the Freemen of Bristol was held.[43]

Maps of the Village neighborhood show very few streets through the nineteenth century. About 1900, the now familiar warren of streets on either side of North Street was set out much as it is now.

WATER AND UTILITIES

Catherine Casey, born in the 1860s, remembered that water was provided to residents from a pump at the corner of Fitch Avenue and North Street. It was brought in by pipes to central cisterns downtown.[44] Farms had their own sources of water from wells and streams on their property.

It makes one consider how the development of essentials that we take for granted in twenty-first-century life were established, when and under what circumstances.

Bristol's modern-day volunteer fire department was developed out of the way that water was distributed in the nineteenth century. When the Rock Spring Water Company was formed sometime from 1880 to 1890, it distributed water by pipe to tubs along the street, as Catherine Casey recalled. This was known as the Munsill system. The water itself came down from Hogback Mountain and then later springs north of the village.

Before that, water had come to the village for seventy-five or more years first by wooden, and then lead, pipes, all using gravity. When lead pipes proved to work poorly, the town experimented with clay pipes, which had been working well for nineteen years when Munsill wrote his history. The pipes were made in the bottom of a ditch; they used a round stick to make a hollow around which they poured their mortar of water, cement lime and clean river sand.[45]

Before the current system of water distribution emerged, municipal solutions were sought. Apparently, there was a certain trial and error in building the water supply, as Gertrude Lathrop told it. When the new system was put in, she said, it was because the old system had become inadequate and the town was compelled to buy water. So craftsmen were brought in to install a reservoir system:

> *They got it all connected and* [got] *a contract for the reservoir, but they didn't say it had to hold water so when the water came down* [into the reservoir], *down it went. And the road was blockaded below the village to where the Lord's Prayer Rock is. So* [the town] *had to get another reservoir to be built and I guess that* [contract] *said it has to hold water.*[46]

Today, water is successfully delivered to the Village through an underground system from the reservoir operated by the Bristol Water District.

MANUFACTURING BEGINS

"But here manufacturing establishments began to spring up…bringing workmen to the scene, and in their wake came shops, stores, etc., which, with the central location to give them permanency, made the village, as it now is, the metropolis of the township."[47]

Manufacturing added to the farming base of Bristol's economy, first in the creation of gristmills, sawmills and forges. As Smith notes, the concomitant industries and shops, to provide for established and new residents and factories as they expanded, blossomed in the downtown.

Stan B. Cushman in his shop on East Street (1910). *Courtesy of the Bristol Historical Society.*

The town grew in these early days and with it the expansion of the largest industries in town. The late 1880s, after the Civil War, however, brought the greatest growth and prosperity to the town. Part V describes how.

TELEPHONE AND ELECTRICAL POWER

The decade of the 1890s was one of growth both in the populace and in the structure that served them.

Bristol's telephone system was installed in 1895. The first switchboard was operated out of the home of Daniel Monroe, whose daughter Josephine was its operator. They lived at 25 Church Street. Josie Pecor, as she was later known, continued to work in telephone companies for about twenty years. The service was offered to subscribers for one dollar per month.[48] Businesses on Main Street immediately began publishing their phone numbers in newspaper ads.

Telephone wires and electrical poles show a very modern downtown (1897–1912). *Courtesy of Thomas Wells.*

From the Monroe home, telephone service grew. Other companies started up, and one prosperous and well-advertised firm was the Bristol Telephone Exchange, also begun in 1895, which operated out of Dr. Bisbee's Village Drugstore. This also was paid for by subscribers. In 1905, the Monroe switchboard was moved to the drugstore as well.

Other firms grew up in the same district and later went to dial service, discontinuing the use of operators, and were bought out by larger concerns developing into the system owned by Champlain Valley Telecom.

George Smith remembered the phone number at his father's store when he was a child during the Depression. It was 133. George Tyler's family had a three-party line. Tyler's number was 82R, and the neighbors' were 82S and 82T. Tyler lived in the Village, and Smith's grocery was on Main Street.

Just how people connected to the operator varied and perhaps changed when a new company took over. At the store, Smith said, "We had to ring. We had to crank it once for the operator." At the Tyler home,

> *We'd just pick it up and the operator would come on. We didn't have to do any ringing. At my grandmother's, you picked up the phone and if no one was talking you'd put the phone back on the receiver and you would crank it just once. And what that would do was drop down a little metal thing so*

LDP&T Company, located in Rocky Dale, was operated from 1897 to 1912 by W.N. Hughes (circa 1890). *Courtesy of the UVM Landscape Change Program and the Bristol Historical Society.*

> *they could see that line was open. That's how they would know* [that you wanted to place a call].[49]

In that same exciting decade, electricity came to downtown. The first power plants were built at Rocky Dale, by the twin bridges. The first of these was owned in part by T.S. Drake, but fire destroyed it in 1897. A second plant was built closer to the road and operated from 1897 to 1912 by W.N. Hughes, who later built a third plant with a longer falls, having a one-hundred-foot drop. Eventually, Bristol's facilities became incorporated within the Central Vermont Public Service Corporation, which now provides the town with power.

The critical moment for the town, however, in this period of expansion and prosperity for Bristol, was the turning on of the lights downtown, along Main Street, in the shops and hotels. That switch was thrown on December 23, 1892. Homes were wired some time thereafter.[50]

Streetlights weren't installed until later, on September 20, 1893. According to Peveril Peake, "Royal writes [in his diary] 'The streets were full of light,'" but not in rural homes until the 1930s.[51]

When electricity first came to her rural household in 1935, Gussie recalled the excitement. It must have been the same for every Vermont child. She was in high school, walking home late from school, and saw the house ablaze with lights. "It was just such a thrill to see. The whole house was lit up and I couldn't wait to get home," she said. "[T]here was just a pull chain in every room, no real switches and no outlets." She was choked with tears, a feeling that came out every time she told the story throughout her life.[52]

The Dunshee Block still stands. Kimball's and Bristol Cliffs Music are located here (circa 1880). *Courtesy of the Bristol Historical Society.*

RAILROADS

Even before electricity and phone service began in 1892, the Bristol Railroad had begun operations.

The arrival of the Rutland and Burlington Railroad in the Champlain Valley in 1849 made regular mail service possible, delivered from the depot at New Haven Junction by stagecoach.[53] That served the town until J.J. Ridley and Myron F. Wilson, who started the *Bristol Herald* newspaper, made a plan to enhance transportation of both goods and people directly to Bristol.

They incorporated as Bristol Railroad Company and opened the six-and-a-half-mile stretch called the Bristol Vermont Short Line. Among the commodities transported in the early years were coffins, syrup and potatoes.[54]

Alan Kilbourn's father remembered using the line to bring grain and other supplies to the Kilbourn Brothers Feed store. "When grain came in, they unloaded at New Haven Junction [for short-term storage]." Later the grain would be brought into Bristol—"Just a single car, with no passengers."[55]

Building Bristol Short Line (1892). *Courtesy of the Bristol Historical Society.*

The Bristol Depot in its heyday (1890s). *Courtesy of the Bristol Historical Society.*

BRISTOL RAILROAD

TIME TABLE No. 86

Taking Effect September 29, 1924.

Trains going west.				On Week Days only.				Trains going east.
5 P. M.	3 P. M.	1 A. M.	Miles	STATIONS	Miles	2 A. M.	4 P. M.	6 P.M.
4.00	12.05	7.45	0	Lv. Bristol Ar.	6	9.15	1.10	5.15
4.17	12.22	8.02	4	New Haven	2	8.58	12.53	4.58
4.25	12.30	8.10	6	Ar. New Haven Junc'n Lv	0	8.50	12.45	4.50

PERCIVAL W. CLEMENT,
President

H. R. BARNEY,
Superintendent

Bristol Short Line timetable (1924). *Courtesy of the Bristol Historical Society.*

Born in Vergennes in 1924, Jack Selden took pride in being brought home to Bristol on the railroad when he was three weeks old.[56]

It ran only until 1930, thirty-eight years. As a three-year-old, Peveril Peake, the last of the descendants of Seth Peake, was on its final run. The trip from Bristol to New Haven took eighteen minutes but much longer returning uphill and fully laden with freight cars.[57]

RELIGIOUS ORGANIZATIONS

Churches in Bristol were strictly separated from town responsibility and authority. In the late 1700s, the Baptists organized first, followed by the Congregationalist, Methodist and Advent churches. It is interesting that the separation of church and state in this area varied from common practice in adjacent villages. Other town governments considered providing meetinghouses as within their purview.

In these early days, churches were established by a handful of local people who created a charter for themselves, sometimes based on the preaching of itinerant clergy. Services were held in private homes or on a makeshift pulpit on the Park. Money to hire clergy was given by members. Some lacked the formal structure of large churches until the joint building of a meeting hall, which they used according to a schedule. In 1819, three churches joined to build such a hall.[58]

The Catholic church, Bristol Academy (later Bristol High School) and the Baptist church at the north side of the park. The school building now houses offices and a gym (before 1900). *Courtesy of Jim Cunningham.*

Religious communities represented a social core for many people, for others it provided their spiritual center and ordered their week and for still others churchgoing was nonexistent. Strict Baptists in Bristol, called "hard-boiled Baptists" by some, kept the Sabbath strictly, allowing no reading except for scripture or Sunday school books, no sewing or other needlework and no entertainments like fishing, games or play. Their lives revolved around prayer: scripture every morning, prayers at night, a weekly prayer meeting and Sunday service. Other families went to church on a regular basis, like the Methodists, without the daily worship.[59]

SCHOOLS

"Bristol has good schools…This is a factor in the life of a growing town which cannot be over-estimated…[T]he town derives great benefit on that account."[60]

Education was an early priority for the first settlers, once the community began to support a population of any true size. Munsill commented that "while none of the early settlers…were men of Liberal Education…verry few, if any, were so illiterate as not to be able to read with a tolerable understanding and write a plain legible hand and had some knowledge of the simple rules of Arithmetic."[61]

Schools were scattered throughout the town in the different neighborhoods. The early town fathers took pride in their schools. They were the first public buildings to be established and served many purposes. The first log schoolhouse was followed by two others in short order, all built with volunteer labor and materials. They were organized by citizens for their own children. The first school in the village was similarly organized, with instruction provided by Anna Rogers, a widow, in Noble Munson's barn. This was in the summer of 1809.

Districts were organized starting in March 1792, and an act approved in 1850 clarified the obligations of the town in supporting the premises and teachers. The town raised money for the payment of teachers through taxes, but the students' families supported the school by providing fuel for heating, as well as boarding the teachers in their homes. Since the 1830s, some funds had also been available to towns from both the federal and state governments for the support of schools.

In the winter, a male teacher was hired for three to four months; a female teacher taught for four to six months through the summer. The first school on the Flats was taught by Dr. Joseph Cable and Harvey Munsill before arrangements for professional teachers were made.[62]

The girls at school were sometimes seen as having the advantage over the boys because the girls' education was uninterrupted. The boys from the farms often had their lessons disrupted by work at home. At sugaring time, the schools wouldn't close, but the boys had to be out gathering the sap and working in the sugarhouse for days at a time. The same was true of harvest time in the fall after school had begun.[63]

By 1886, the town had nine school districts. The Bristol Scientific Institute had been established before the Civil War, after which it became the Bristol Academy. The named changed again in 1881 when it "was organized as the Bristol Graded School."[64]

It "was removed a hundred rods to its present location about 1876," that location being at the corner of the Park.[65] From that time, it was known as Bristol High School.

Gertrude Hewitt Lathrop was sent into town to school even though there was a school in her district:

> *I was supposed to go to the Flats School, but Mother had been to a local school and when she got to high school she had to get boarded and she didn't know anyone. So she arranged for me and my sister* [to go to school in the Village]. *We went just one year and then went to Bristol High School. We weren't supposed to ride the school cart. We had one mile to walk. It didn't hurt us any. In fact, it was good for us.*

She graduated in 1930.[66]

Today, children living in the Village still have to provide their own transportation to Mountain Street School and to Mount Abraham, but often it is by car rather than on foot.

Not everyone in town was able to go or to finish high school for one reason or another. And some people were illiterate, especially the poor French Canadians or Irish who came to work or farm. Well into the twentieth century, so much depended on a family's means and circumstances. Gerald Heffernan's grandmother "could only read a little and write a little bit," having to go out and work as a girl.[67]

Among those who were unable to finish their schooling was Sam McKinnon. In 1927, he left school to work. He and his twin sister, Alice, had been brought up by different grandmothers, and at that point he was determined to go out on his own.

For those who didn't finish high school, said George Smith, "It wasn't because they couldn't." That is, it wasn't because they didn't have the aptitude. "It was because they got interested in other things."[68]

McKinnon hadn't felt deprived and declared that he "got as good an education as anyone," nor was he a snob about his life-lesson brand of schooling, recognizing the value of a diploma. He had been invited by his classmates to attend the high school reunions over the years, but he declined, saying "Not until I get a diploma." He had wanted to go to one of the reunions in particular at one time, because there was a classmate attending, Lloyd Sykes, whom he'd known and would have liked to meet up with again. But he wouldn't go unless he had that diploma. So it never happened.

Many years later, decades later, someone mentioned to Sam that all he needed to get a diploma was to go down to the high school in Middlebury and take an exam, which he would surely pass. He had a friend at this time who taught in Middlebury, and Sam asked him about the exam. The friend, who turned out to be the one who administered the test, knew that Sam would easily pass. However, he never did it, remarking in later years that it was something he had continued to regret.[69]

HEALTHCARE AND MEDICINE

Medicine in times past, as it is today, is made up of both informal elements and the professional medical structure of doctors and hospitals, nurses and midwives.

Bristol has been well served by resident physicians, however, since its beginnings. The list of the earliest physicians recorded a Dr. Joseph Cable as early as 1794. One of his patients was bitten by a rattlesnake and survived to quite an old age. A pair of twins, Henry G. and George H. Sumner, had been out berry-picking. They returned home in the Bristol Leg and discovered that a rattlesnake had come with them. Henry reached toward George to give him the stick that he was carrying so that George could kill it, and the snake snapped up and bit his finger. He discovered the bite only when it began to bleed profusely. Dr. Cable was called in but not before the poison's effects constricted Henry's throat. Nonetheless, and despite a great loss of blood, Henry survived, dying in 1856 at the age of eighty-four.

Throughout the town's history, including those early years, more than one doctor practiced simultaneously, so people had their choice of a physician. Along with Dr. David Bosworth, their names are among the familiar names of the town: Hasseltine, Allen, Hall and others.

Anson Norton, a local boy, became a doctor in the town and is remembered for his dedication during the influenza epidemic of 1918–19. He was also active in local political life. Francis Briggs, both a surgeon and general practitioner from the 1890s until his death in 1924, was known as much for his music as his ministrations.[70]

Before the supremacy of the current biomedical system began to dominate in the early 1900s, doctors were commonly homeopaths. Bristol had at least one, Dr. E.I. Hall, who practiced during the 1880s and '90s.

Two physicians shifted professional gears to become pharmacists. In the 1860s, E.M. Kent opened the South Side Drugstore on Main Street, a name retained until at least 1980 as part of the Rexall Drug chain. D.A. Bisbee opened the Village Drugstore later, in the early 1880s.

Other medical specialists came through the towns of Addison County in a way similar to traveling entertainment. The papers ran announcements of the arrival of a dentist or optician, such as W.B. Guy, an optician from Saratoga, New York, who made himself available to potential patients at the Bristol House in June 1900.[71]

Today, the Bristol Rescue Squad is another facet of the town's medical services. Dr. Harry Roller was largely responsible for its start in the mid-1940s, along with Gordon Brown, the undertaker. Dr. Roller had been taking his own patients to the hospital by putting their stretcher in the back of a car. Both he and Brown recognized the need to stop relying on Middlebury and Vergennes's ambulances or Dr. Roller's setup. Brown had some training in first aid and in operation of the equipment, so he began an ambulance service. But it wasn't until 1970 that the Rescue Squad itself was formed.[72]

ORGANIZATIONS AND CLUBS

Bristolites have always had a number of social organizations and committees in which to participate, both men and women. In the past, this gender divide often marked the boundaries of membership. But all such clubs contributed lasting gifts to the ongoing life and rhythm of Bristol.

The Library Association, before the library was built, was a favorite activity of women of the town. Both wives of W.A. Lawrence were active in it before their early deaths.

The Entertainment Association and the Village Improvement Society were early local organizations whose missions were to make Bristol an attractive place in which to live. The former sponsored entertainment, but the latter engineered plantings in the Park and initiated other beautification projects.[73]

The Outlook Club had its origins in 1900, when it was a literary society, soon changing its mission to "promote general culture, an intelligent interest in the leading questions of the day—national and international—and community improvement."

It was this club that organized the 1921 pageant to celebrate Bristol's history, Chautauqua courses for both children and adults and formal lectures and concert performances in town. Since 1940, the Outlook Club has written and updated a history of Bristol and continues to be involved in community action, for example during Red Cross blood drives.[74]

Political organizations also had well-attended meetings, and gentlemen were identified by their membership in both the *Bristol News* reports of their activities and in the biographical sketches of Hiram Carlton in 1903.

"Mr. [William S.] Howden," Carleton wrote, for example, "is a Republican, and he has bestowed a due share of attention on the affairs of the party."[75]

The note about the Munsill family at the end of Munsill's history records both Harvey's and Newcomb's political affiliations. Judge Harvey was "a frequent presider at political conventions, both Whig and Republican, and was active in matters of reform, especially temperance…He served efficiently as chairman of the Republican county committee and had been widely considered as an available candidate for the [New York] Assembly judge."[76]

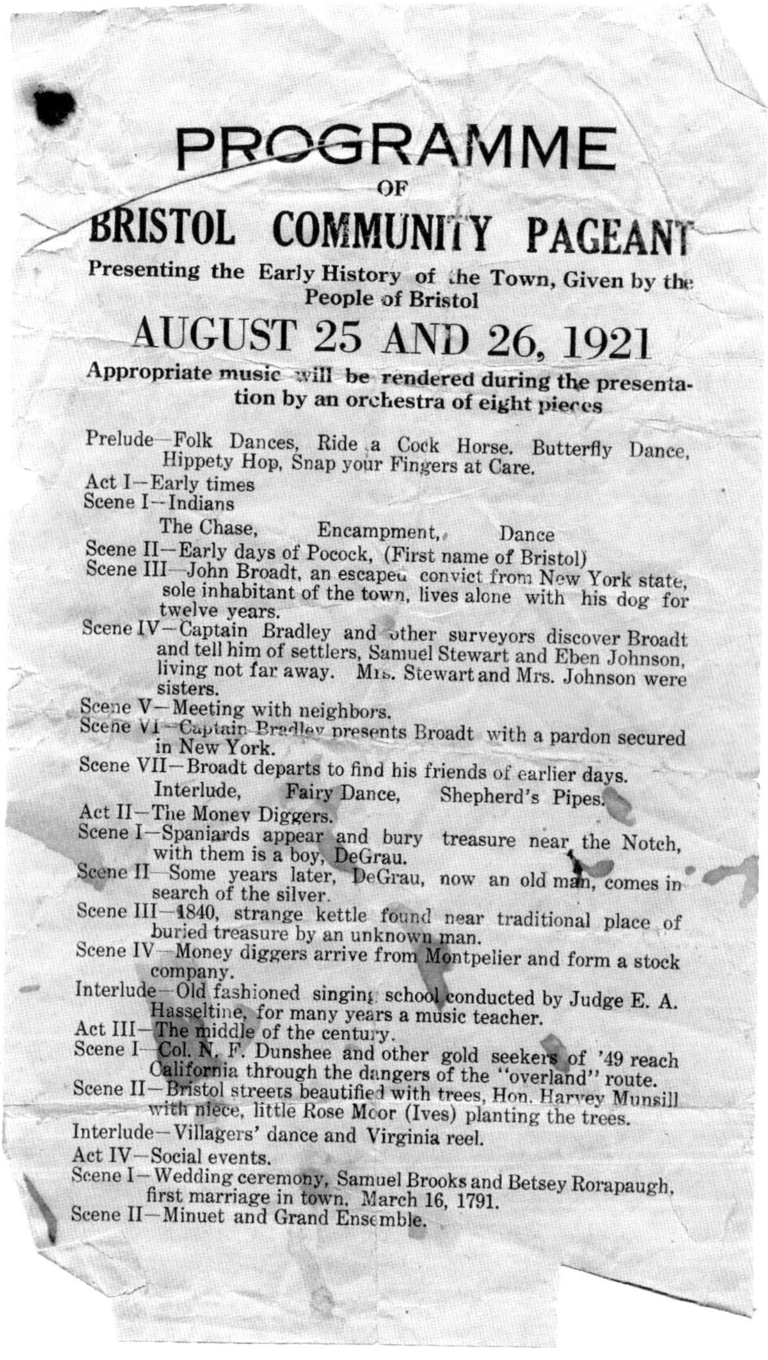

PROGRAMME
OF
BRISTOL COMMUNITY PAGEANT

Presenting the Early History of the Town, Given by the People of Bristol

AUGUST 25 AND 26, 1921

Appropriate music will be rendered during the presentation by an orchestra of eight pieces

Prelude—Folk Dances, Ride a Cock Horse, Butterfly Dance, Hippety Hop, Snap your Fingers at Care.
Act I—Early times
Scene I—Indians
The Chase, Encampment, Dance
Scene II—Early days of Pocock, (First name of Bristol)
Scene III—John Broadt, an escaped convict from New York state, sole inhabitant of the town, lives alone with his dog for twelve years.
Scene IV—Captain Bradley and other surveyors discover Broadt and tell him of settlers, Samuel Stewart and Eben Johnson, living not far away. Mrs. Stewart and Mrs. Johnson were sisters.
Scene V—Meeting with neighbors.
Scene VI—Captain Bradley presents Broadt with a pardon secured in New York.
Scene VII—Broadt departs to find his friends of earlier days.
Interlude, Fairy Dance, Shepherd's Pipes.
Act II—The Money Diggers.
Scene I—Spaniards appear and bury treasure near the Notch, with them is a boy, DeGrau.
Scene II—Some years later, DeGrau, now an old man, comes in search of the silver.
Scene III—1840, strange kettle found near traditional place of buried treasure by an unknown man.
Scene IV—Money diggers arrive from Montpelier and form a stock company.
Interlude—Old fashioned singing school conducted by Judge E. A. Hasseltine, for many years a music teacher.
Act III—The middle of the century.
Scene I—Col. N. F. Dunshee and other gold seekers of '49 reach California through the dangers of the "overland" route.
Scene II—Bristol streets beautified with trees, Hon. Harvey Munsill with niece, little Rose Moor (Ives) planting the trees.
Interlude—Villagers' dance and Virginia reel.
Act IV—Social events.
Scene I—Wedding ceremony, Samuel Brooks and Betsey Rorapaugh, first marriage in town, March 16, 1791.
Scene II—Minuet and Grand Ensemble.

The events program for the 1921 Bristol Pageant organized by the Outlook Club. *Courtesy of the Bristol Historical Society.*

A party for L.E. McShane, soon to leave for World War I. *Front, from left*: Ira Norton, Don Wilson, Bill Roach McShane and Clement Burnham. *Rear, from left*: Reuben and Cardell Norton, Martin Rider, David Bosworth and V.I. Patnode (1918–19). *Courtesy of the Bristol Historical Society.*

Newspapers did not claim to be objective, as they do today, but rather identified themselves with a party. The *Bristol News* described itself as "a clear progressive weekly newspaper…Politically the *News* will be a staunch supporter of the Republican party."

In Bristol today, it is not something that people make much of; it is common instead to avoid political conversation until one has established a relationship.

Membership in fraternal organizations was similarly cited. The Bristol Lodge of the International Order of Odd Fellows (IOOF) was established in 1898 with 26 charter members, quickly growing to 145. The Masons were here from 1826.[77]

Dr. Briggs, for example, was a "member of the Phi Chi Medical Society, and is prominently identified with the Masonic order, being a member of the Libanus Lodge and Gifford Chapter, of Bristol and Mt. Calvary Commander, K.T. of Middlebury. He is also identified with Bristol Lodge and Encampment, Independent Order of Odd Fellows, being past chief patriarch of the latter body."

A modern postcard showing the Park decorated for Cool Yule, an annual celebration of the winter holidays (2008). *Courtesy of Thomas Wells.*

W.A. Lawrence is described after his marriages and children thus: "In fraternal relations he is prominently connected with the Mason order, being now a member of Mount Sinai Temple of the Mystic Shrine of Montpelier, which he represented in the grand conclave at Boston. He is also a member of Bristol Lodge, No. 36, I.O.O.F."[78]

"…As a Mason he [the Honorable Harvey Munsill] was master of Libanus Lodge…from 1836 to 1866…And held the charger during the anti-Masonic movement."[79]

Even William S. Howden's affiliation with the Masons was noted, even though he himself was not a member of the fraternity: "Mr. Howden was reared, so to speak, in a Masonic atmosphere, his father being a Mason of high degree."[80]

An Onawa Rebakah Lodge was established in 1900 and the Libanus Order of the Eastern Star, in 1901. These gave women the opportunity to contribute good works with goals different from the Outlook Club.[81]

These organizations were visibly involved with town affairs or provided the focus of social interaction and affiliation. They provided funds for municipal projects and for promoting values, such as temperance. Until recently, one of the most colorful and unique traditions of Bristol, the Fourth of July Outhouse Race, was organized by the Rotary Club, as was the decoration of Main Street for the winter holidays. The Rotary, begun in 1951, was recently disbanded.

Most of the Bristol branches of the fraternal clubs closed as late as the 1970 and 1980s, others only recently.[82] During their day, they were responsible, however, for services that are now provided by churches, the town and business owners' groups like the Five Town Council, part of the Addison County Chamber of Commerce, and Bristol Downtown Community Partnership.

Except for Florence Cragen's experience, little has been recorded of the part that these organizations played in the personal lives of their members.

Part IV

The Life Cycle of a Village

Saturdays we always made bread.

—*Gussie Levarn*[83]

DAILY ROUTINE

In the past, household chores and routines were usually organized by Mother by the days of the week. This rhythm changed after World War II. Monday was wash day, Tuesday was for ironing and on Wednesday the mending was done. On Saturday nights "you bathed in the kitchen washtub."[84] And every week began with church on Sundays.

George Smith and George Tyler both recall that Mondays were wash days, too. Gerald Heffernan recorded that his mother "made bread on Wednesday and Saturdays. And also when she made the bread, she made Parker House rolls that we would have Saturday night with baked beans with a slab of salt pork in it."[85]

The main meal was dinner, enjoyed at noontime, whether in town at the Bristol House, the family home on Spring Street or out on the farm. A big breakfast was had after chores on the farm or at about 6:30 a.m. The boys and hired men were awake by five o'clock in the morning with Mother already having the fire going and oatmeal on the stove. For everyone, the evening meal was supper, a lighter meal, something heated up (leftovers) or sometimes even just sandwiches or cake.

Gussie Levarn's childhood home was run like that. Like Laura Ingalls Wilder, living on the prairie just sixty years before her, Gussie spent evenings darning, knitting or mending. It was the way the household kept everyone clothed and warm. "You didn't have four or five pairs of pants like the kids have today," she said.[86]

Before and during the Great Depression of the 1930s, Mother made the children's clothes except the boys' pants, which were store bought. She would make shirts for the boys' and the girls' dresses. Socks were repaired by the hearth, whether they were knit at home or purchased. Growing up, said Tyler and Smith, they only had one good shirt to wear to church on Sundays and one pair of good pants.[87]

The town had its own rhythms of celebrations and town business. The tradition of town meeting is one of these. It has been held on the first Tuesday of March since 1854.[88] Another is the arrival of news of the outside world and how it spread throughout the village. Personal news, the mail, was catch as catch can in the early days. As Munsill tells it, before 1803 "a few letters and the Middlebury Mercury [newspaper]...was carried to Bristol by arrangement made by a few of the early settlers among themselves to go and get the mail...from Middlebury, each one taking his turn and in that way the mail...was received each week."[89]

Once a post office was established, first at Daniels Corners and later in the Village, delivery was regular. However, it initially arrived once per week on horseback, then twice a week and finally coming every other day until the arrival of the Rutland and Burlington Railroad. Once that had been established, mail came twice a day, being brought from the depot at New Haven Junction by stagecoach.[90]

The news of the village and that of the outside world, brought by traveling salesmen or other visitors, was shared at the Bristol House at the corner of North Street and Main. Men of the town convened there for socializing every day, much as the Old Farts Club does in 2009. Such gatherings were a means of voicing opinions about the direction of town events and governing policies as much as of spreading the news.

Still other patterns in town life are represented in its celebrations, like the Fourth of July. In Bristol today, Independence Day is celebrated with the Outhouse race, a parade and fireworks, following a long history. It is one of the largest parades in the state, often graced by candidates for statewide public office.

Some of the specifics have changed over time. The schedule for July 4, 1900, included first the parade, then a 1:00 p.m. concert and speeches at 1:30 p.m., followed by races. These included one-hundred- and two-hundred-yard bicycle races, two-hundred-yard foot races, a hurdles competition and potato and sack races for fun. A band concert was given from 7:00 to 8:00 p.m., followed by fireworks and "a promenade concert in Holley Hall in the evening after the fireworks."[91]

Celebrations of Old Home Week. Note that the flag only has forty-eight stars (1912). *Courtesy of the UVM Landscape Change Program and the Bristol Historical Society.*

THE GREAT DEPRESSION

The Depression, which began with the stock market crash of 1929, was a hard time for the country as a whole, of course, and it played out in this small Vermont town whose economic height had passed. Throughout the country, farm communities weathered the Great Depression more easily than more urban places. That seems to have been true for Bristol and surrounding towns.

Gussie Levarn told of her mother packing barrels of food to send to her sister May, who lived with her husband in New York City. May's husband had a job with the railroad, but still her mother sent down potatoes, carrots and canned goods like corn, jellies and jams. They were big barrels, fully packed, and her father took them to the train station to be taken south to the city.

Another memory is of Gussie's mother making bedsheets out of grain bags. She would "wash them and put them outdoors in the sun and bleach them out." The old Yankee adage "Use it up, wear it out, make it do, or do without" was especially true at this time, with rural families having the advantage because they knew how to do much with little.

Most Bristol people seemed to feel that they didn't suffer any particular deprivation. Most people who recall that time in their childhoods say that "we were no more poor than anybody else." Nonetheless, some tell of going to bed hungry, as did Gussie's husband Rosie, remembering a childhood of little food and still less variety. Others speak of the plenty on their families' farms—milk, butter, cheese, eggs and foods put up in the summer for winter use. That was what made some families better off. Gussie's family sent two girls to college and Gussie to nursing school during this era.[92]

People became creative in provisioning for their families, for example bartering what they had for what others could offer. George Tyler's father went house to house outside the Village to offer fresh bread or pastries. He was known as "the bread man." In return, he would bring home berries or eggs. Sometimes, the berries he got from one household could be traded or sold at another, at other times his mother would put them up in jams and jellies.[93]

Gertrude Roscoe Bingham tells of the men staying at her mother's boardinghouse bringing fish in from the river. One day, Mrs. Roscoe came down in the morning to find a bathtub full of bullhead. She also received squirrels and rabbits to make into pies. In the Depression, people sold what they could—if they had chickens, eggs would be on sale—but also wild blueberries, horseradish and other things were sold door to door to bring in some money for the family. Often it was the children sent out to sell in this way. And, of course, the heat and the cooking came from wood fires.[94]

Fancy birthday cakes were not common in Bristol, at least for ordinary folks. An especially wonderful treat for Mrs. Roscoe, who ran the boardinghouse, came on her fiftieth birthday. Her daughter, Alice, and her husband came down from Burlington. The son-in-law was a Frenchman, and it was he who brought the surprise of a store-bought decorated cake with yellow roses created from icing. For someone making daily meals for everyone else and in great numbers during hard times, this must have been a truly wonderful treat.[95]

If they had the money, parents would sometimes buy treats for the children, or Mother would make cakes, cookies and other goodies. A well-known treat was what some called rag muffins. Maple sugar was blended with butter and spread onto baking powder biscuit dough to be rolled up like a jelly donut, cut and baked. Fried dough was a fairly universal Depression treat—pinches of dough dropped in hot oil to be popped in the mouth, still warm.[96]

Gussie Levarn described store-bought treats brought home by her father when he went to Burlington to do the big shopping, buying the big sacks of bread flour, white and brown sugar and other staples that would keep them stocked at home. On one occasion, he brought home honeycombs so they could have honey on their baking soda biscuits at suppertime. Another such surprise brought home from a shopping journey was a string of bananas. They were neither as cheap nor as plentiful during the 1930s as they are today.[97]

Before the days of hospitalization for delivering babies, Gussie said that her mother "used to go and help deliver these babies up there to Martins'. One year they had two."[98]

The bread and milk poultice, or mustard plaster, was a common home remedy. There were many ways in which medical problems or illnesses were treated at home because of the lack of a doctor.[99]

Notwithstanding the generous supply of medical professionals from the earliest days, as those who have lived through the Great Depression have recounted, it was not always affordable to call the doctor.

When people were sick, as often as not things were handled at home by the family, even in particularly difficult times, like the smallpox epidemic in 1934 (described in part seven). Many people had books like Gussie's mother's, which described illnesses, their cause and how to treat them.

The home pharmacopoeia that led Mrs. Bostwick to use sulfur to sterilize her letters during quarantine was not unusual. During the smallpox scare, she would place any letter she had written in the tines of a fork and put it in the steam rising from a pot of sulfur being kept heated on the stove. Then she slipped the letter out the kitchen window to a box, where someone would fetch it to the mailbox or take it to the postman.[100]

There were other home remedies or measures taken. For example, Helen Bosworth, of the notable and well-educated Bosworth family, ate whole garlic during the winter months to keep from getting the viruses common during the cold season. It was said, "Of course nobody would get near her during the winter" because the scent of the garlic followed her.[101]

There were other reasons and other authorities. In days past, going to the doctor wasn't the only way to cure an ailment. Sam McKinnon was healed of a painful growth on his finger through the influence of spiritual agency and through prayer. Traveling with his wife up to Quebec, they stopped at the St. Ann de Beaupre shrine on Isle LaMotte on the way home and purchased a crucifix. His wife put it away on a bureau, where it stayed. Then Sam got a growth on his finger that just grew and grew no matter what he did. Getting "so sick of it," he saw a doctor, asking if it were a wart. He was told that it was not, though the doctor didn't know what it was. Sam went for a second opinion, but this doctor didn't know what the growth was either but made an appointment for Sam at Mary Fletcher Hospital for the following Wednesday.

After work that day, he went right upstairs and got the crucifix down, saying "prayers, lying my hand on the crucifix which was lying on the bed." Without telling his wife about it, he worked again through the Tuesday, and as they discussed the next day's appointment, Sam "happened to put [his] hand on the table, just casually like this and she said 'My God, it's gone!'... It was completely gone."[102]

MUSIC AND ENTERTAINMENT

"I can remember sliding down the hill behind the Wissel house in the Winter time, going on hikes up to the 'Ledge'...[b]and concerts on Thursday nights...and the movie theatre."[103]

Entertainment has always been found at the various formal venues in town, outdoors, through sports and at home. Much special entertainment was brought into town or arrived of its own volition from across the country and even farther afield. In 1900, strolling musicians were seen on the streets of Bristol. The *Bristol News* tells of a bagpiper who arrived, followed by the visit of an Italian musician, complete with organ and monkey! Bristol was a stop along their regular performance circuit.[104]

Other public amusement was arranged by the Bristol Entertainment Association, whose mission was to provide formal programs. These were often held at Holley Hall but also other venues such as the Bristol House, Dike's Hall and more, but for a ticket price. They even sold season tickets.

Occasional special events brought entertainment to Bristol, too. During the eighteenth annual encampment of the Son's of Veterans in the summer of 1900, a parade and evening dance at Holley Hall were open to the public for the admission price of five cents. The public was invited to welcome and celebrate the visitors by decorating their homes along the parade route.[105]

Free events have often included the local band playing in the Park. The Bristol Town Band has provided weekly summer concerts since 1870, also giving citizens a social venue (for both band members and the audience), as well as an outlet for creative talent. It provides something of a symbol of the town in the covered bandstand on the green. This is especially true for those from away who experience Bristol as a stereotypical, or "picture postcard," New England village.

Like many town bands, the Bristol Band originated with the return of Civil War veterans who had played in regimental units. It was begun by Smith Hatch, who directed it for about fifteen years, members wearing uniforms and the group having a military bearing. It was called the Hatch Club at that time. The band played at baseball games as early as 1883 and officially became the Bristol Cornet Band. Throughout the 1880s, the group played at all sorts of local functions, including ice cream socials and bicycle races. The band itself sponsored two or three bicycle races each year and named the winner.

The Bristol Band has been playing weekly summer concerts since the Civil War. The bandstand is dedicated to Roy Clark, who became director in 1955 (2008). *Courtesy of Carol Wells, Bristol Downtown Community Partnership.*

In 1886, part of the group had split off into the Citizens Band. Both bands played in town on the same night, alternating tunes and playing from different venues. One played at the west end at the Bristol House, the other on the steps of the Hatch Block at the east end of Main Street. The two recombined in 1895 as the Bristol Military Band. However, a subset of players formed a ten-piece orchestra to play at dances, socials and parties, including Middlebury College dances, the balls at the Union Block and at the Addison County Fair. The entire group, with new military-style uniforms, played at Smith Hatch's funeral at Holley Hall in 1896 and at the opening of the Champlain Bridge in 1928, when John Selden was band director.

The bandstand was an open-air stage until 1937, when the roof and acoustic ceiling were added. For many years, this was the best-constructed band shell in the state, with other town representatives coming to Bristol as recently as 2003 to use it as a model for their own.[106]

Town baseball was another favorite pastime. There were many teams from as early as the 1870s. The most recently formed club was the Bristol Softball League, started in 1979. Through the years, different teams were organized,

The Bristol baseball team. *Back, left to right*: Walter Dagget, Miles Stanis, R.W. Peake, Theodore Wells and Henry and Hoyt Landon. *Front, left to right*: Will Dagget, captain and pitcher; Kelley Hatch; Wilder from Northfield; Dick Smith Constable; and Watson and Doug Drake (1892). *Courtesy of the Bristol Historical Society.*

including a semiprofessional team. Long before that, though, baseball was played on the floodplain on the south side of the river and later on the field where Mount Abraham Union High School now stands.

During the period from 1910 to 1917, an enterprising man by the name of Flagg, from Brandon, rented Holley Hall one or two nights a week to show movies with equipment that he brought with him. Later, Bristol had its own cinema, the Colonial Theatre, located right on South Street. Built in 1915 by George S. Farr, it was a busy gathering place for townspeople until its closing. Silent films were shown two nights a week, with a piano player providing the background music in the early years. The rise of cars, taking people out of Bristol for their entertainment, was cited for its demise.[107]

Other school-based activities included the drama club, the Beta Sigma Society, the Glee Club—in which George Smith sang—and Future Farmers of America.

One of the things that opened up as an activity with the advent of the automobile was Sunday trips out into the countryside. George Tyler, whose

COLONIAL

Bristol, - - Vermont

PROGRAM WEEK OF MAR. 3

Sunday - Monday Mar. 3-4

DOORS OPEN THIS SUNDAY AT 6:00 P.M.!

Charles BOYER

Lauren BACALL

In

"Confidential Agent"

Also

"A Square Deal for Every Child"

Exhibited for the American Legion and dedicated to the children of Veterans.

Wed. & Thurs. Mar. 6-7

A Fantasy in Color

"Yolando and the Thief"

FRED ASTAIRE LUCILLE BREMER

FRANK MORGAN

Friday and Saturday Mar. 8-9

"Senorita From The West"

ALAN JONES BONITA GRANVILLE

"Cuban Madness"

Chapter IV "JUNGLE RAIDERS"

The Bristol Press, 17 Maple St., Bristol, Vermont

Colonial Theatre program (1945). *Courtesy of the Bristol Historical Society.*

family lived in the Village, remembers family day trips with picnics in the car. "Practically every Sunday from the Spring through [Fall, we would] go to different places in Vermont…to Island Pond or Newport, places like Hyde Park. Those were places I remember visiting. My mother and father wanted us to know that there were other places besides Bristol, and we'd put up a picnic and head out and get back at seven o'clock at night."

George Smith agreed. "That was a big thing in those days—picnics. My folks used to go visiting. We'd go over to Bridgewater. And we'd go to the cemetery and see where relatives were born."[108]

Roller skating and weekly dances were other favorite activities, involving both young and old. The Japanese Garden, complete with hanging lanterns, was built in the mid-1920s by Harry Jimmo at the corner of Liberty and West Streets. The introduction of dancing was inspired, some say, by Jimmo hearing someone remark that his recently lain hardwood floor would be wonderful for dancing. The Garden had a reputation for having the best dance floor in Vermont. It was a center of entertainment and socializing before World War II but eventually closed in 1947. Before its closure, however, the owners removed the "Japanese" from its name to set a new tone, distancing it from association with the current national enemy.

There were wonderful, open sides to the building so that when the bands played people could hear from outside as well as dance inside. The Bristol Band often played at these dances. The open sides invited those not dancing to park and enjoy the music from their cars.[109]

There was also entertainment to be had at the back of Wendel's barbershop upstairs at the top of Main Street, where Cubber's now operates. As a teen, Jack Selden was there. "I spent a lot of time in the backroom...That was where the pool hall was." But there was another place to play in town, too. "Dick Thomas had a pool table there. It was a big shift coming down to play pool at *this* house" (referring to the Maples, also known as the gingerbread house, on Hewitt Road).[110]

Horsemanship has been a form of entertainment as common in the Village, where Juna Perlee lived, as on the farms. Juna was a lifelong horsewoman to whom the fenced-in riding ring on Liberty Street is dedicated. She was often seen riding in town and in Fourth of July parades. She also shared her knowledge, both formally and informally, organizing the Bristol Riding Club in 1955.

Nellie Martin remembered a more unrestrained equine entertainment. When she was growing up, young men would ride down into Chase Hollow or Fuller's Flats to race horses for a lark.[111]

Families also visited one another on winter evenings till late at night to share news, enjoy music and dance and to have parties. In the long, dark winter, people visited in their homes. There were sliding parties where hot chocolate and sandwiches were served to guests and sometimes cakes and cookies, too. A drink of syrup with sugar and cocoa and water might be served. Friends would bring sleds and some had toboggans. And, of course, there were sugar-on-snow parties in the early spring, as the bright sunny days helped bring people out of the winter's self-imposed hibernation.

Martin tells of skating and sledding parties happening where she lived on Fuller's Flats. "We had very good sledding…They used to go up from Bristol to our place…There was quite a little knoll, and we'd go up into the woods and come down through. And at the bottom we'd have skating parties. We used to have a lot of fun."[112]

In the summer, people held socials and served homemade ice cream. Making ice cream was inexpensive for farm families because they had their own milk, eggs and cream.

Gertrude Hewitt Lathrop lived out on Hewitt Road. "On Sunday in summer time, we made ice cream. My mother would go out and skim off the milk cans to get the cream. We'd have strawberry ice cream, raspberry. Dad liked that—we all did."

The Thomas family lived across the road. "They had six children. The oldest, a girl, was six months younger than I was. We went to high school together. She had five brothers. I used to go over in the evenings and we played games. I was always over there on Saturday afternoons."[113]

Georgia Bostwick was a teacher. Among the first things she did to celebrate having her first job and an income of her own was to buy a second-hand radio. That made the family popular in the community, with the neighbors from along the road joining them to listen. "[T]hey'd come over at night and listen to the radio…to *Amos and Andy*…all the chairs all around in a circle in front of the radio."[114]

Radios became more commonplace and were often a cause for gathering and listening as a group, as happened at Mrs. Roscoe's boardinghouse. One resident had a radio in his room when *The War of the Worlds* was broadcast on October 30, 1938. One of the residents had heard at the garage that Martians had landed so everyone crowded around his radio to hear. There were comments on the air from people who had supposedly seen it.

The bubble burst when Pinky Russell, who had been at his uncle's, the dentist Dr. Grissom, had heard that it was nonsense—"just a Halloween story" as he put it. As the boardinghouse residents were glued to every word coming from the speakers, Pinky arrived to tell them the truth.[115]

With the entertainment of radios and television emerging in individual homes, other forms of entertainment declined. There was a period in the early 1950s of waning membership so the town band combined with the Vergennes Band, giving concerts in each town. When this disbanded, the Bristol group started up again, still playing Wednesday night concerts every summer. Similarly, sugar-on-snow parties, ice cream socials and other means of gathering in one anothers' homes have all but disappeared.

Noah Lathrop stands by the third team of horses in this lumber caravan. As a child, Florence Cragen enjoyed watching them (1915). *Courtesy of the UVM Landscape Change Program and the Bristol Historical Society.*

For a young Florence Cragen, watching normal happenings in the village was entertainment enough. She loved watching the logs brought in from surrounding towns down on Mill Hill at the lower end of South Street by the sawmills. When that happened, great loads of logs were stretched the length of Main Street, waiting to be taken off the wagons.

Another particular joy was going to the railroad station to watch the trains arrive. Cragen recorded joining Helen Bosworth, when they were just village girls, in many of her activities. They often played house "in the old-style coffins" at Bristol Manufacturing, the casket factory owned by Helen's family.[116]

At Lathrop's sawmill below the Village, the log piles were stacked high beside one of their buildings. Jack Selden and his friends enjoyed climbing up the log pile to the roof and jumping off it into the river. "They'd spot us up there, me and Percy Bussey…[and yell at us] 'Get off that roof!'"[117]

As adults, the Bosworth sisters, Helen and Grace, lived in the family home at 1 Park Place. They are often spoken of with great fondness many, many years after their deaths more than fifty years ago. At one point, Helen was a Girl Scout leader, but they were also known for inviting children to play badminton, set up at the back of the property.[118]

The Lawrence Memorial Library was a place where children went too, as much for socializing and the activities held there as for the books. Two of the librarians were particularly well liked: Mrs. Irish, who served for many years, from 1928 to 1933 and again from 1939 to 1949, and Lee Landon's mother, Lois, who served from 1933 to 1939.[119]

Still later, when comic books ruled, Park Filling Station was a common hang-out because the comics were sold there, and it was a handy stop along the walk home from school for George Smith. For Jim Atkins, who lived in Bristol as a boy from 1945 to 1955, Sam McKinnon's, where his father worked, was the preferred hang-out. Other favorite places were "Jewel's 5 & 10 cent store...George Lathrop's Sporting Goods...Tudhope's Grocery, Snap's Restaurant...[and the] skating rink."[120]

Atkins recalls living on South Street, next door to the Colonial Theatre and above Brown's Funeral Parlor. From age eight to eleven, he helped the ticket taker at the theatre seat people on Saturday nights. It was common practice at the time to tip the staff for seating you, and the ticket taker was generous enough split his tips with Jim.

His favorite swimming holes were off East Street—one was right by the Lord's Prayer Rock, which generations have climbed and used as a slide, and another called "Elliot's" was further on.

The "Church Street Gang" included the many Davignon children in the 1960s and '70s, as well as the Dearborn, Hanson, Abbott and Clodgo families. Patrick Davignon, who lived at 29 North Street, recounts a closeness among the neighborhood families similar to that Laurie (Desorda) Darling recounts of her life on East Street from the same era.[121]

Part V

Land Use Tales: Milk, Mills and Wood

The river provided the source of power for the sawmills, the iron forges and the grainmills, basic goods needed to build and sustain an community, the dense forest provided the lumber to build a settlement and the raw material for the many wood industries that laid the foundation of the town, still thriving 241 years later.
—*Cindy Eaton*[122]

The combination of the Flats and surrounding agricultural land, a good water supply and mill streams, as well as the surrounding forests that could be harvested for high-quality wood, proved ideal for a place like Bristol to prosper during the era of its settlement and well into the twentieth century. Bristol has had a mix of the three since its early days, and the related industries, while considerably changed, still provide the basis for Bristol's existence.

FARMS

Bristol is largely an agricultural town. Its first residents farmed for their subsistence, and commercial dairy farming followed when refrigerated cars were first introduced by the railways. Farms not only raised crops for consumption or for their dairy herds, some crops also brought in an income of their own. Large quantities of the early cash crops raised in Bristol were shipped to Boston and New York via the Rutland and Burlington Railroad.

Today there are few farms right in the Village, the Four Hills Farm among them. Most remaining farms are on Bristol and Fuller's Flats and northward toward Monkton. Most are now commercial entities, selling milk to the larger dairies and production facilities, to be distributed throughout Vermont and nationwide. Large factory trucks now take the milk from local farms on a daily basis, but it wasn't always so.

According to Gertrude Lathrop, there were thirty to fifty working dairy farms on the Flats during her childhood in the 1920s and '30s. And they all had to have hired help.

She said of her parents, "Oh, my folks worked so hard." She described some of the activities on the farm at various times of year, including maple sugaring. Her father tapped three maples near their house, "some down back of the pasture, and he rented three on Bristol Flats near the school house. He rented those and up in the Notch he rented [other maple stands]. There was a lot of running around…It was a busy time of the year."

They also made caked maple sugar for sale. "We had a table and put a metal top on it. And if we had orders…[some from as far as] California, he would make the boxes. There were huge kettles you got to a certain temperature and there was a wooden paddle to stir with." The wooden boxes would hold two-pound sugar cakes. They used galvanized tin dividers to cut them into smaller units. A single-pound block would make eight two-ounce cakes. "We had nice white boxes to fit, to deliver them in."[123]

In 1956, the Coffins bought the 342-acre O'Neil farm on Monkton Road. Sylvia and her husband raised Holsteins. The O'Neils had owned, farmed and rented out the land since the 1800s. The Coffins were just the second owners of the property, and Sylvia recalls the extensive title search to trace through all that time.

When Silvia and Leonard retired from farming and moved to their newly build home across the street, most of the acreage was sold to Four Hills Farm. Other acreage was sold to a private owner (twenty acres) and to Vermont Bicycle Touring. This is how many of the large tracts of farms that were once within village limits were broken up into smaller plots of land.[124]

Dairy farming created a need for creameries, the first being Cold Spring Creamery, began in 1897 by Evarts and Eastman. It prospered enough to build a branch creamery at New Haven Mills in the adjoining town. The Riverside Condensed Milk Company was built near the creamery, Evarts and Eastman later taking over that concern also. The firm was closed in 1901, with the creamery and condensed milk factory sold at auction. The new owner, Mike Hannon, later sold to woodworkers Hewitt and Wright. Another creamery, Odell's, operated from 1903 to 1905.

Some of the neighborhoods of Bristol were informally named after farms and farmers. The crossroads at the base of Stony Hill where Route 116 joins Route 17, for example, is called Daniel's Corners or Daniel's Four Corners. The Daniels farm was once situated there. Likewise, Fuller's Flats and Chase Hollow, both lying along the stretch of Route 116 between the Village and Starksboro, are named for nearby farmers.

The Odell creamery at Cold Springs about 1903–5. The man in the photo is the owner. *Courtesy of the Bristol Historical Society.*

Today, farms like New Leaf Organics, north of the Village on the Monkton Road, sell at the Wednesday Farmer's Market on the green and elsewhere. Some are based on organic methods of raising vegetables, eggs and flowers. Others, not organic, base their livelihood on providing local produce, which is highly prized these days. Their products are sold also at local shops and to the restaurant industry, as well as to individuals through CSA programs, in which members pay ahead of season for a share of the yield.

There was once even an agriculture course at Bristol High School and a school farm. According to Jack Selden, "Mass[achusetts] Agricultural College came to Bristol to teach aggie classes. The school farm had potatioes, corn, apples trees, cherries. Dan Thomas did that. We'd go up there and he'd pick cherries—three cents a quart."[125]

RIVERS

The New Haven River, flowing behind the downtown area and through much of the farmland in the Flats, and Baldwin Creek have been actors in the life of Bristol as much as any pioneer, local character or famous author. There might not have been a town, certainly not one with Bristol's character, otherwise.

From the mundane, like providing opportunities for sport fishing and driving the many mills in Bristol and neighboring New Haven, to the floods that often put people out of their homes and livelihoods, washing away small firms as well as farmland, the rivers are critical to the story of Bristol.

The dominant role of the New Haven River in Bristol's history, however, falls to the building of mills from the first days of settlement. Sawmills were built first and continue to figure importantly in Bristol's economy. Munsill records that the first sawmill was built by Amos Scott, followed by the first forge. Other sawmills were quickly built in every neighborhood lying adjacent to the river, including one on Baldwin Creek.

The gristmills were busy well into the twentieth century. The earliest was built in the south of town on Bristol Flats at O'Brian's Brook. Feed and grain, for both human consumption and animals, was essential.

Famously successful among these was one owned by Enos Soper, along with a brother and a third partner. Soper, who was "a skilled mechanic," according to Munsill's papers, spared no expense to build a highly competitive enterprise at a time when there were many such small firms. Others flourished or lived short lives through the vagaries of fire and flood. Among the casualties of the flood of 1869 was the Stewart gristmill at the base of Mill Hill, making way for the building and expansion of Bristol Manufacturing.

The mill owned and operated by the Kilbourn family shaped village life in many ways, from the end of the nineteenth century until the 1960s. It began on East Street as a grain and feed store established by Arthur B. Kilbourn and E.W. Smith in 1896, the former buying out his partner in 1900. By that time, the Cyclone Gristmill had been built on Main Street, where it stands today. The mill purchased and processed grain from local farms. In the twentieth century, the company began to sell farm equipment, garden supplies, hardware and kerosene. In the 1960s, the name changed to Kilbourn Brothers, owned and operated by the founder's sons after the death of John in 1968. The family continues to be proud that on its closing it had been the oldest family-run business in Bristol history, operating for seventy-two years.

Major mills and wood manufacturing concerns were located here to take advantage of the good, fast-flowing waterways that the New Haven River afforded. Where neighboring towns like Lincoln and Starksboro remained fully agricultural hill farming communities, Bristol had the advantage of the river. It continues to be the reason for Bristol's place as the center of the five towns, including also Lincoln, New Haven, Starksboro and Monkton.

Bristol Manufacturing Company. *Courtesy of Thomas Wells.*

Kilbourn's Cyclone Gristmill. Since its closing in 1969, the building has had a variety of tenants and uses. *Courtesy of the UVM Landscape Change Program and the Bristol Historical Society.*

The river also provided a household commodity that was essential for many: ice. It was part of a farm family's work to harvest blocks of ice from the frozen river every winter. On the farm along Hewitt Road, the Lathrop family fished for trout and cut ice where the river flowed nearby. "I can remember going out there. They would score the ice and then cut it. They had a ramp they moved the ice up and as one layer would fill up, they'd cover it with plenty of sawdust on it and make another layer and move the ramp up. They had four or five layers."[126]

WOOD

Bristol has been all about wood since the beginning, from the introduction of sawmills and the manufacture of wooden items early on in the town's history to the current lumber companies.

The mills centered on the processing and manufacture of wood products. These businesses provided the mainstay of the town's economy, supporting all the other industries in the town, including the retail concerns on Main Street and the medical, dental and other professional offices. Only the dairy industry was independent of it. However, the two were complementary in supporting the town. Farmers with woodlots were the start of it all.

In the 1880s, Noah Lathrop opened a sawmill in the Notch, which prospered until 1925. His son, William, carried on the tradition nearby, but his grandson, Clarence, moved the operation into South Bristol in 1935. Local firms like Drake, Smith & Company transformed the lumber into manufactured goods sent around the world. The Lathrops moved operations to Waltham when forested land was scarce but returned to the South Street location in 1947 under Claire Lathrop. Claire's own sons (Jim and Tom) remain in the lumber business today. They are joined by A. Johnson Company, which came to Bristol in 1938.

Apparently A.L. Cain found himself unemployed at the end of 1898. He had the notion that there was money to be made in the manufacture of small wooden items, specifically from the birch trees that were locally so plentiful. That November, Cain broke ground at the corner of Pine and Maple Streets and built the Bristol Novelty Company in the upper story of its own small sawmill. He began with ten to fifteen employees making, according to the *Bristol News*, "hair pin or pill boxes, whip sockets, bicycle handles, pipes or almost any article a machine can turn to wood." Also according to this newspaper account, by 1900 the firm had grown to more than fifteen workers, most of them women.

Still using a two-person saw, a tree is felled and cut by Guy Blaise (back to the camera) and an unidentified man (1950s). *Collection of the Henry Sheldon Museum, Middlebury, Vermont.*

There were four women who fit the lids to the boxes, "scouring and packing them ready for shipping…Upstairs [on the main floor], another ten or more women worked the machinery."

The newspaper declared proudly that the Bristol Novelty Company shipped out over seven thousand pipes per day at the turn of the twentieth century.[127]

The future of the firm became bound to that of the New Haven Manufacturing Company, which had lost its factory to fire in 1912. The Town of Bristol negotiated with the latter to come to Bristol to reestablish itself, which it did, becoming the Vermont Box Company. By 1954, the company was committed entirely to building furniture, the demand for wooden boxes having diminished. The firm's name was changed to Drake, Smith & Company, Inc. It was selling furniture throughout New England and beyond, operating a retail store on Main Street during the 1970s.

There were many small manufacturing industries in Bristol in the 1860s, the height of Bristol's economic well-being, but by far the firm that made the most impact, both at the time and in enduring ways, was the Bristol

Bristol Manufacturing Company at its height of financial success between 1890–1930. *Courtesy of Jim Cunningham.*

Manufacturing Company. In the latter half of the nineteenth century, it was the single biggest firm in town.

In 1870, a handful of men opened a company to manufacture doors, sashes and blinds, known by its owners' names as the Howden, Bosworth Company, with W.S. Howden as president. The timber came primarily from their own lumber mill along the New Haven River. There were twelve men on the payroll.

The small enterprise that started at the base of Mill Hill on South Street became a tremendously successful business. In 1877, it added coffins to its inventory and became the Bristol Manufacturing Company, continuing to grow so that by 1900 there were 110 to 120 people employed, as well as 5 men on the road selling the company's products. It became the largest casket-making firm in the country.

The Bosworths were involved with the company from the very beginnings until its closing. Bristol Manufacturing operated, in one form or another, for seventy-seven years, from 1862 through 1939. By its final days, the complex was a huge landmark.

The casket factory was a cornerstone of community and industry. As Bernard Bosworth, the Reverend David's grandson, records, Bristol Manufacturing provided more than merely jobs for locals and summer fun in the millpond. The company supplied standby electricity when the town's electric facility at Rocky Dale lost power and organized a fire-fighting group.

Workers at Bristol Manufacturing Company at the turn of the twentieth century. Note the women in the center of the picture. *Courtesy of the Bristol Historical Society.*

Dr. Bosworth spoke of the other families whose lives were wrapped up in the Bristol Manufacturing Company as much as his own. Bernard was the grandson of the Reverend David Bosworth who, in 1867, joined the partnership of William S. Howden and Benjamin Daggett by purchasing the third original owner's share. Bernard and his brother, Nichols, ran the company in its last years until its closing in 1939. Among those workers he remembered decades later were Ethel Johnson and Liza Kingman.

Lime kilns represented a short-lived industry in Bristol (1860–1900). *Courtesy of the UVM Landscape Change Program and the Bristol Historical Society.*

Sumner and Prime manufactured beekeepers' supplies, and the Bartlett Plow Manufactory and even a clothes dryer factory operated in Bristol. Still other businesses were those of blacksmith, joiner, harness maker, carpenter and shoemaker. Lime kilns were an early industry in Bristol, though the lime available in other parts of the Champlain Valley, being of superior quality, soon dominated the market. Furniture was made here by both Drake, Smith & Company, later, Deerleap Furniture. Specialty furniture is still built in small artisan workshops, as are pottery and other crafts.

From 1948 to 1967, the VanRaalte Company, which manufactured women's nylon underwear, thrived here. Though it employed a large number of Bristol women, it was not a homegrown firm.

From 1943 to 1959, Kennedy Brothers, now located in Vergennes, operated on Mountain Street, where once the Bristol Trading Post and now Phoenix Rising is located. They specialized in woodware and manufactured pottery.

The entrepreneurial spirit remains lively in Bristol, but manufacturing has become a very small part of today's Bristol economy. On Main Street, Vermont Honey Lights makes beeswax candles behind its retail shop, but other manufacturing concerns are scarce.

During the 1970s, Kevin Harper created Autumn Harp, and Paul Ralston started the Vermont Coffee Company in the 1980s. Such incubator businesses continue to start up, and some succeed, just as the Bristol Novelty Company did in the late 1800s.

Autumn Harp's product lines have changed through its life, just as they did for Bristol Manufacturing and Drake and Smith. Originally focused on natural baby products—nonpetroleum jelly and baby powder—Autumn Harp shifted to lip balm and lip gloss in the 1990s, which it produces and packages for other brand-name firms. That firm continues to operate at the site of the former Drake, Smith & Company factory on Maple Street.

While Vermont Coffee Company has flourished across the state and beyond, both of these newer companies have had to leave Bristol to find space for their growing operations—the coffee company to Middlebury in 2008 and part of Autumn Harp to Essex Junction.

MERCHANTS AND THE DOWNTOWN

"Our Merchants are now selling goods as low as they can be offered, and as good purchases can now be made in Bristol Village as at any other Village."[128]

In 1797, Robert Holley opened Bristol's first store on the Flats, selling a wide variety of goods. Seth Peake was the first to operate a store in the Village itself. He had set up trade first as a harness maker, with skills learned from none other than Robert Dunshee. Upon moving into the Village, though, Peake opened a dry goods store. In 1819, Winter Holley began selling goods within the Bristol Hotel. At that time, the hotel was owned and operated by Winter Holley's father, Robert, who had expanded his own livelihood from farmer/shopkeeper to innkeeper.

George Parmalee owned first a drugstore, then a dry goods business. He was, for a time, in partnership with Alvin U. Stewart in selling books and groceries but later became sole owner. This shop was located on the corner of South and Main Streets, opposite the Bristol Hotel.

Abraham Gaige had holdings on Main Street in which others ran their businesses, such as George Parmalee and William G. Munson, who partnered in business at one time with both A.P. Roscoe and someone named Barber. Similarly, Willis Peake held property downtown. In 1988, his Village home was featured in the film *The Wizard of Loneliness*.

Ice carts brought blocks of ice through the Village. Nellie Martin tells of her childhood in the 1880s when she and friends would follow behind these carts hopeful of getting a chunk of ice. Ice that was for sale was cut from Lake Winona (Bristol Pond). It was cut and packed with sawdust in icehouses for keeping until the peddler would travel house to house.

Bristol's current marketing rack card displays a modern version of this same view (1880–93). *Collection of the Henry Sheldon Museum, Middlebury, Vermont.*

North Street in the 1950s; the Bristol Inn is front right, Mrs. Roscoe's boardinghouse next and the Peake House beyond, behind the trees. *Courtesy of George Vince.*

The delivery wagon of N.J. Hill. *Courtesy of the Bristol Historical Society.*

The Bristol House, with J.J. Ridley owner, undertaker and initiator of the Bristol Short Line Railroad. *Courtesy of the UVM Landscape Change Program and the Bristol Historical Society.*

The Commercial House and Bristol House, at either end of town, were built to accommodate visitors. Their owners operated other businesses from those premises. Later, the former, known as the Hatch Block, housed both a mortuary and a furniture shop. Ridley, of the Bristol House, was, as noted in part three, an undertaker like his competitor and also behind the introduction of the Bristol Short Line.

There were stables in town one hundred years ago, attached to other businesses or as their own going concern. One place was located "at the corner of Pleasant and North Street…and over on West Street right at the corner of West Street and Maple there was another livery stable," where now, appropriately enough, a gas and service station is located.

Dorothy Trudo remembered Clinton Grover's stable. "He didn't have but one arm. I don't know how it was taken off but he had a laundry and a stable out back behind the school, behind the [Baptist] church. When I was going to school…But it didn't last very long. The cars began to come, so he didn't continue."[129]

Livery stables and harness shops did robust business in this era (1880–1900). *Courtesy of the UVM Landscape Change Program and the Bristol Historical Society.*

5/A
WE SELL
Horse Blankets

From the days when other early settlers moved into the Village either away from farms or to add operating retail and service businesses to their livelihoods, the downtown district has been vibrant. There were public houses and funeral parlors, mercantiles and hardware stores, farriers and feed stores. Shops sold farm implements, household supplies, home furnishings, clothing and food, produced on outlying farms for sale to the townspeople, and every other kind of goods people required to raise their children, run their homes and make a living.

Unlike many surrounding towns, Bristol is only partially a bedroom community. Much of its economy in 2009 still relies on the three basic resources found here: farms, rivers and woodlands.

Part VI

Bristol Women at Work

The females who were among the early settlers of Bristol acted well their part; deprived as they were of many of the Comforts, and almost necessities of life they were found to be the pattern of industry and economy; proud of the management of their own domestick affairs they did not disdain to be found, under pressing necessities by the side of their husband and father or brother in the field assisting them to secure their hay and grain.
–Honorable Harvey Munsill, Esq.[130]

As Munsill wrote, Bristol women have always been a part of making the town successful. It is that wonderful Yankee industriousness that both men and women share that while there were officially men's and women's work, boundaries were crossed when necessary. At other times, of course, women took jobs by choice, preference and enterprise.

ON THE FARM

Initially, the residents worked for their own subsistence, branching out into commercial businesses and cash crops soon thereafter. Among those chores taken up by women were to card, spin and weave their own fabric from flax grown on their own land.

Most families living on the farms were large. Gussie Levarn's own family had eight children: Mary, Flora, Georgia, Rick, Carleton, twins Bill and Gussie and Juna. As soon as a girl was old enough, she was mending her own and the brothers' clothing. In Gussie's home, even the girls worked the farm chores with their father—"Juna loved it"—so women's work was primarily left to Gussie and her mother.

Gussie Levarn tells of her father taking the kids out to do farm work as soon as they were able to. Her mother told Gussie that when her father took her out to the barn to learn to do chores, she was to act incompetent and she'd soon be sent back inside to do housework. This made Gussie happy because she preferred cooking and caretaking to farm chores anyway. And so it went. Gussie pretended she couldn't figure out milking cows, so her father dismissed her and she was back making cakes in no time.[131]

TEACHING

Most of Bristol's teachers were women, and many of them were local, even in the early days, an era of primarily male teachers. The first teacher in the village was a woman (see part three). Rosie Levarn's mother taught school, and Gussie's older sister, Georgia, taught in Bristol.

George Tyler's mother became a teacher before she married. "There was a plea that they needed grammar school teachers." She was only an eighth-grade graduate, never having gone to high school, but she was trained to become a teacher, along with Alice and Mary Dalton.

Grade school children and their teacher in front of Holley Hall, late 1880s. Holley Hall was used by the school for a gym and for all-school gatherings. *Courtesy of the Bristol Historical Society.*

Tyler continued:

> *They took the train from New Haven to Rutland, and they were met by horses and carriages from Castleton Normal School—this was on a Sunday afternoon—and they spent that whole week cram-coursing to become teachers…If my mother hadn't married she probably would have taught her whole life, like Alice did.*[132]

Nellie Martin's aunt, Catherine Casey, taught in Bristol, Monkton and Starksboro around the turn of the twentieth century. "She was a very good teacher," Nellie believed. She taught "the Weaver boys, my brothers, the Sugarette boys, the Lamb children."[133]

HOTEL WORK

Catherine Casey also did hotel work. "She taught school and in the summer she had to work because the pay was so small. She worked summers in the hotels." However, one year Catherine couldn't go to her hotel job because she had to care for her own father, who was ill. One summer, Nellie Martin "went over to Hotel Champlain because Aunt Catherine couldn't go. I went in her stead…John Tyler's half sister had been down there for several winters, and I worked [there for] four years."

The staff of an unknown Bristol business, perhaps one of the hotels. *Courtesy of the Bristol Historical Society.*

Nellie also went out of state. "[O]ne summer I went down to Kearsarge, New Hampshire, and then four summers in Michigan." She met her husband there.[134]

Gerald Heffernan's grandmother left school early to take a job making beds at the Bristol Inn.[135]

NURSING

Libby Cushman and Gussie Levarn were nurses in the service during World War II, along with other Bristol women. Gussie had always wanted that career, one of the few open to women. She was a caretaker, she said, from early on, preferring housework with her mother to working the farm. When she graduated from high school at seventeen, she was not yet old enough to enter nurse's training and so spent a year "as a nursemaid" to her uncle's children in Boston. She returned to take a course in biology at Bristol High School, a requirement for admission to nursing school.

When she finished her training at Mary Fletcher Hospital in Colchester, Gussie went overseas. One of her most-remembered experiences came at the end of the war, during the liberation of the concentration camps. She recalled the horrific state of the prisoners. After the war, she did hospital nursing, working at Porter Hospital in Middlebury.[136]

BOARDINGHOUSES

Mrs. Varney owned the boardinghouse on North Street, opposite the Bosworths', and Gertrude Roscoe Bingham's mother acquired it when Mrs. Varney retired. It was there that Gertrude lived with her widowed mother and five siblings. There were some local regulars that took meals at the boardinghouse, though they lived elsewhere. These included Mrs. Briggs, widowed in 1924 with the death of Dr. Briggs. She came to dinner regularly, impressing Gertrude with her jewelry. William Cardell, the dentist's father, took his meals there, too. It is said that he would go down to breakfast at the boardinghouse, go into the Village and visit with people at Park Filling, across from the green, until noon. Then he would return for his midday meal. He then went back up to the Norton's, returning again for supper.

The work of feeding and providing daily necessities and housekeeping services for both residents and diners was accompanied by other tasks, like sending children to the shops, dealing with emergencies (like the two deaths

Gussie Levarn during her nursing service in France during World War II. *Courtesy of Cheri Rockwood, Snap's Restaurant.*

Blanche Marsh operated this boardinghouse for handicapped children. The house was once owned by Colonel Noble Dunshee. Howden-Hall is on the right (1930–56). *Collection of the Henry Sheldon Museum, Middlebury, Vermont.*

that occurred there) and accommodating workmen at three to a bed when workers came to repair the roads after the 1938 flood. These men went home on the weekends but stayed in town during the workweek.[137]

Still another boardinghouse matron was Blanche S. Marsh, who operated from 1930 to 1965. Her charges, however, were handicapped children. Her home on West Street, moved back from the road in 1956 to accommodate the building of Park Filling Station, had been the home of Noble Dunshee.

Gussie tells of her sister, Juna, taking boarders into her home. It was a viable opportunity for women to make a good income but not take them out of the home, and it would require no extraordinary skills, as most girls learned them while growing up. It was something that Nellie Martin attempted but, she said, "I couldn't make a go of it."[138]

In 2009, this remains a means of making extra income for homeowners in the Village, as housing for those taking courses at Phoenix Rising Yoga Therapy or the overflow of tourists at particularly heavy times.

MANUFACTURING

Many women worked at Bristol Manufacturing, right from its earliest days through the 1960s. Catherine Casey worked there for a year. Nellie said that female workers were paid "seventy-five cents a day for a year before you could get a raise."[139]

Women represented the greatest number of employees at VanRaalte and continue to be very largely represented at Autumn Harp.

The VanRaalte Company made high-end lingerie, stockings and underwear for women, the fabric being woven at other VanRaalte facilities. Those with children were lucky to find child-care in town. Libby talked about taking her son up the street to Mrs. Bingham's and paying fifty cents per hour for babysitting, which reduced her wages considerably. VanRaalte rented space in the Tomasi Block on the south side of Main Street in 1948 and continued to operate into the 1960s. Many Bristol women sewed for them. Lottie Follonsbee was a supervisor, and both Libby Lattrell Steadman and Gertrude Bingham were among the employees.

There was a base pay of fifty cents per hour plus a percentage based on how easy or difficult the item was that a woman was working on. The pay was based on the minimum that would be required to simply meet one's production quota, an overage being paid for extra output. Libby's favorite was making lace, which also was the most lucrative piece to be working on if you were good at it, and she was. Lace making was considered more difficult so Libby "made production" easily and the extra percentage as well. Seaming pants was considered easy, so workers would have to stitch the seams of many more pairs of pants to surpass quota.

However, she said, a lot of workers didn't make production. Libby also explained that if workers consistently exceeded production, the company reassessed and increased the quotas. Before the company closed its Bristol plant, people were paid by hour at the minimum wage. Both Libby and Gertrude remember that they had to work hard there.

The workday at VanRaalte included lunch and rest breaks, of course, but the freedom of the workers to take their break outdoors in front of the building was curtailed. The Bristol Inn still stood across the street in the 1950s, and visitors would often wonder about the workers taking a cigarette break along the sidewalk. It was commonly assumed, and often asked, if the building housed a woman's prison. When the company heard about this, they forbade the workers from taking their break outdoors.

Other factory jobs were available to women, too, and Libby also worked at the Vermont Box Company, which she particularly loved, enjoying the scent of the wood. She also enjoyed the people she worked with, which, she said, was what made a job a good job in her estimation. Later still, she worked for Simmonds Electronics in Vergennes.[140]

WOMEN'S WORK IN OTHER ARENAS

When her husband died in 1906, Alma Curtin wrote up his notes and papers for him. She also wrote his memoirs, published in 1940.

Office work—formal and informal—typically was and remains a woman's occupation. Many Bristol farmers' wives, for example, act as the family firm's bookkeeper. "Mrs. Peake…used to be a bookkeeper at the Burlington Savings Bank. That's where Royal Peake discovered her."[141] Two of Alice Dalton's sisters went to Washington, D.C., at the beginning of World War II and worked in government offices.[142] Josie Pecor, Anna Bissonnette, Ruth Norton and others were telephone operators.

Florence Cragen owned and operated the Ben Franklin store with her husband John. Miss Dumas, "a small lady trained by the Dunshees," managed their retail shop on Main Street. "She groomed Warren Brooks" to be a shopkeeper; he eventually ran his own business.

George Tyler's mother took in laundry when he was a boy. They lived right in the Village. When the German School was in session, he said, "She could only take in seven or eight of the laundries these men and women needed to have done. She didn't have time. There was no place to hang" more than that.

She also sold corn and potatoes grown right on Maple Street. "One of us boys would have to be home if somebody wanted to buy corn or potatoes. The corn was ten cents for a baker's dozen…[She] always had enough to pay taxes and to paint the house every three or four years."[143]

Part VII

Fire, Floods, Disaster and Death

"On October 26, 1898 came the big fire...[O]*ver half of the business section on the north side of Main Street was destroyed."*

–Bristol News[144]

FIRES

The Great Fire of 1898 and the extensive 1924 fires are said to have been the worst in town history because of the amount of the downtown destroyed. The 1947 fire devastated the Bristol Manufacturing Plant on South Street, which after years of decline shut the firm down for good. In 1974, another fire devastated parts of Main Street, resulting in the closing of businesses that had operated there.

"In 1924, a great fire started from a harness shop of South Street, spreading to the south side of Main Street, gutting most of the buildings, and completely leveling the grist mill [Cyclone Gristmill]. The mill was quickly rebuilt with a second structure to be used as the office."[145]

In a recounting of the history of Bristol and Danforth Company, the *Bristol News* listed the products saved from that fire before the building burnt to the ground: "33 pairs of ladies' shoes, seven of mens', $600 worth of rubber goods and the watches and rings in a safe." Because they were well insured, "the firm was the first to rise from the ashes...November 1, there were ready to receive customers" on the second floor of the Masonic Hall.

Of Bristol and Purinton, described by the paper as a "young mercantile firm" selling men's boots and shoes, it described the fire as interrupting sales for a few days but that firm, too, rebounded quickly, having saved most of its stock. It had enough insurance to cover its losses and "inside of three days were doing business in the basement of the Town Hall. They stayed there a week

The south side of Main Street after the fire; the fire hose is still in the street (October 1924). *Courtesy of the UVM Landscape Change Program and the Bristol Historical Society.*

The O'Neil Block, the false-fronted building adjacent to the brick one and left of center in the picture, was a landmark and one of the oldest buildings in town until it burned in 1929. McKinnon's Mobil Station followed. *Courtesy of the UVM Landscape Change Program and the Bristol Historical Society.*

The Vermont Box Company manufactured sleighs, wagons, boxes and cabinets for Victrolas (1915). Autumn Harp now stands here. *Courtesy of the UVM Landscape Change Program and the Bristol Historical Society.*

The Drake-Farr Block, Main Street, before the 1914 fire. Business flourished during the mid-1880s. *Courtesy of the Bristol Historical Society.*

The Drake-Farr building after the fire, smoldering, with icicles hanging visible from the eaves (February 1914). *Courtesy of the UVM Landscape Change Program and the Bristol Historical Society.*

and moved into part of Hatch's furniture store." The store was lauded as the only store in Addison County dedicated to shoes and boots, declaring that it probably had the largest stock of its kind between Rutland and Burlington.[146]

Bristol was a growing center at the end of the nineteenth century and as it moved into the twentieth, but the fires that were to come played a role in the town's decline. While not creating the downturn in economic fortunes in and of themselves, the fires and floods of the coming years fueled some already-occurring industry collapses.

It was after the 1924 fire that the bell in the firehouse was replaced by an electric siren, still sounded every day at noon. The inability of the bell to be heard on the night of the fire was due to a heavy wind that dissipated the sound. That, along with the wind itself, was responsible for the fire getting out of control and spreading too rapidly to save the south side of Main Street, including the Cyclone Gristmill. A.B. Kilbourn himself went onto the rooftop to prevent the fire from destroying it. According to Alan Kilbourn, charring is still visible in the basement of the part of the mill that survived.

That fire was said to have originated in a South Street harness shop. The fire bell itself was sold for junk and eventually returned to Bristol, where it was returned to the firehouse tower.

In 1914, the Drake-Farr Block on the south side was destroyed by fire. And in 1929, fire destroyed the landmark O'Neill building, changing the face and character of Main Street. The O'Neill Block, which stood where Sam McKinnon's filling station stood later, had been a hotel at one time and a business block. The National Bank of Middlebury is located there now.

Jack Selden lived in the Village as a boy and related this story. "The fire was heading right for our house so we had to get up. I looked out toward Main Street, and the whole thing was on fire. It was about midnight…I must have been about five. My mother and father were downstairs…It was an inferno!"[147]

FLOODS

Bristol Manufacturing had already lost many of its smaller buildings in the Flood of 1869 when, as Helen Bosworth wrote, "A great cloud burst took away all the buildings except the lower factory…and washed away all the dirt from the island."

That 1869 freshet, as it was called at the time, also destroyed a small gristmill at the bottom of Mill Hill, which then became absorbed into the complex of the growing Bristol Manufacturing Company.

From that experience emerged the cause for a major shift in the company's mission. Until that time the company had not made coffins, according to

Hurricane winds destroy a barn (1950). *Courtesy of the UVM Landscape Change Program and the Bristol Historical Society.*

Huge snowdrifts here along Main Street, but business carries on. Despite the blizzards that have come and gone, none has done major damage in Bristol (1920–40). *Courtesy of the UVM Landscape Change Program and the Bristol Historical Society.*

the last president of the company, Bernard Bosworth. But when the firm recovered from this disaster, their market had been taken over by other, smaller firms, providing sash doors and blinds, its original trade.

After reopening, the firm began making coffins in small numbers in 1870, but by 1877 it became the mainstay and incorporated as the Bristol Manufacturing Company.

In November 1927, flooding destroyed nearby New Haven Mills, as well as many other communities in Vermont. In Bristol, the twin bridges in Rocky Dale were swept away. Also, this flood brought the beginning of the end for railroads, especially the small lines. With the flooding, many were destroyed, while many others, like the Bristol Short Line, lasted only another few years.

The September hurricane of 1938 brought many great changes to the town at an already-challenging time because of the Great Depression and the growing war in Europe. The New Haven River flooded, finishing off many local businesses and washing away the ground beneath them. Locals recall seeing coffins from Bristol Manufacturing stranded up in the trees in its aftermath.

The Great Depression had already rung the death knell for some companies. Bristol Manufacturing was on its last legs, going into receivership in 1936 and closing in 1939. Before the flood, the company had already made great cutbacks, reducing staff hours. This time, the company simply could not rebound, the flood having washed out that entire stretch of river. The company was sold to Perley Eaton in 1939. He fared no better, and the 1947 fire noted above leveled the buildings.[148]

In that same 1938 hurricane, the electric plant at Rocky Dale was destroyed, the successor to the one mentioned above that had been run by W.N. Hughes. Its repair required purchasing land from the Central Vermont Public Service Corporation (CVPS) and rebuilding with the water gate moved. Yet another hurricane came through in 1950.[149]

ACCIDENTAL INJURY

Two brothers, Lawrence and Sidney Moody, suffered in the kind of hunting accident still all too common today (remember Dick Cheney). While hunting deer, the brothers separated in different areas of the forest of the Notch. Lawrence had taken a break and, while sitting on a log, was seen by his brother as he brushed flies from his face. Sidney took it for the tail of a deer and shot Lawrence in the back of the neck. There was no reason to suspect animosity, as Sidney had the wherewithal to recognize his brother and rush him home to get help. While Lawrence survived, he never recovered, being partially paralyzed for the remainder of his life.

Just a few years later, two Bristol militia members were at an exercise, loading a cartridge into a cannon. However, the charge from the previous shot hadn't burned out, so the cartridge exploded immediately in their faces. While they survived, William Haskins's arms had to be amputated below the elbow, and John F. Blass was less seriously injured.[150]

EPIDEMICS—SCARES AND OUTBREAKS

Disease epidemics started to affect Bristol in its earliest years: Samuel and Elizabeth Stewart, the first settled family, lost two children as infants before they arrived, and in 1803, three more (of their total of eight) died of scarlet fever.

Even earlier, in the fall of 1789, however, an influenza epidemic took hold. While it was widespread, no one in Bristol died. That could not be said of the smallpox outbreak first seen in Bristol in 1794 and that killed Cypran Eastman in May 1798.

Dr. Joseph Cable, one of the physicians in town, inoculated many of those known to have been exposed—as through contact with Captain Eastman—as well as other citizens who wanted to be. Those inoculated and exposed were housed in a building called a "pest house," erected by the town to prevent the spread of the disease. It seemed to have run its course shortly thereafter, and normalcy returned.

Smallpox returned to Bristol in early 1820, killing twenty-five-year-old Filavel C. Williams. Williams was not a resident of Bristol but was working as a traveling vendor of men's clothing for a Canadian firm. Like Eastman before him, Williams had infected others before the diagnosis was made, and people became afraid. Again, inoculations were given and a "pest house" was provided.

In 1803, a variety of other diseases affected Bristol, some fatal, others not. Among the deadly ones were scarlet fever, whooping cough and measles, taking children's lives primarily, including Luma, the seven-year-old daughter of Gurdon Munsill. There was an outbreak of influenza at this time that, while affecting nearly every family, caused no deaths.

Further epidemics, in 1810 through 1813, proved very destructive to the population, and many died. In 1810–11, typhus fever was responsible for many deaths. Among these were Manchester and Surviah Holley and Olive Munsill.[151]

Gussie Bostwick (later Levarn) and her twin brother, Bill, who survived an outbreak of smallpox but was killed in World War II. *Courtesy of Cheri Rockwood, Snap's Restaurant.*

In 1812 and 1813, the threat came from "spotted fever," which took the most robust and healthy adults of the community, killing them within hours or days of contracting the disease.

The town was fortunate to escape an 1832 cholera epidemic that killed many in Montreal. One of the town fathers, though, Oliver Chilson, caught it in 1842 while traveling. But Bristolites did not suffer an outbreak and no doubt considered themselves lucky. Ten years later, however, an unnamed disease, whose primary symptoms were that it started in the throat and spread throughout the body, produced a high and deadly fever. Whatever it was, many local people died.

Among those named in the death records for that year, perhaps having died of the disease, were Mandana Rutherford, another of Robert Holley's daughters. She had just remarried after the untimely death of her first husband, Ezekiel K. Dunton, in 1837.[152]

Bristol experienced another smallpox scare in 1900, which turned out to be only chickenpox. Later, in 1934, smallpox again came through the region, as noted above.

At those times when there was no doctor nearby or there wasn't money to call the doctor out, people relied on what experience the family or community had to both identify and treat common ailments. When the smallpox epidemic appeared it was a combination of both that saved the life of Gussie's twin brother.

The way the story is told, when Gussie's brother Carlton became sick, the doctor was summoned and he diagnosed chickenpox. Their mother disagreed. "I've had eight children, and they have all had chickenpox, and this isn't chickenpox" she told him. She sent the doctor to see the boy next door, who was experiencing similar symptoms. He returned in agreement with the diagnosis of smallpox and established a quarantine at their house. Before long schools were closed because so many children in the area were affected.

Bill, Gussie's twin, was then hit by the disease, quickly and severely. When the hired man came in from milking one evening for supper, he told them that Bill hadn't come out to help. He was sent upstairs to the boy's room and found him unconscious. Gussie concluded that his fever was so high that Bill had had a seizure. In any case, the hired man brought him downstairs. Mrs. Bostwick packed pillowcases with snow, using newspapers and a horse blanket underneath (as we'd use a rubber sheet now) and put those around the patient with fever. Though she wouldn't have him back in the house, the doctor later said that had she not brought the fever down with those cold packs, Bill would probably have died.[153]

During that quarantine, there was a certain amount of reasonable fear coursing throughout the district, though no deaths were recorded for Bristol.[154]

DEATH AND FUNERALS

The first death in Pocock was a tragic accident. A small boy was crushed by a tree being felled to clear land. Amze Higby, only four or five years old, had been sent by his mother to call his father, Nehemiah, inside for dinner. The tree that Nehemiah had been cutting had begun its fall just as the child called out. The tree was falling in that same direction, but before his father could get him out of harm's way, the boy had been crushed.

Accidental and tragic deaths have always been a reality for Bristol, as for any other place. Even in the earliest days, suicides were committed. Munsill tells of Elijah Marble, a man believed to be from Warren. In 1831, Marble was discovered dead in Orrin O'Brien's barn in Bristol, on his back on the floor, a gunshot wound in his chest. The inquest, presided over by Harvey Munsill, concluded that the gunshot was self-inflicted because the gun was rigged so that he could fire it with his foot.[155]

Other suicidal deaths include that of one of Mrs. Roscoe's lodgers. The boarder had been unpleasant: "He wasn't a nice man. He didn't like himself, and he didn't like anybody else either I don't think. And he was very argumentative. And my mother said, 'We're a big group here and we have to get along. And if you can't get along then we'll have to make an arrangement.'"

The man went to live with his son for a time but soon returned. Shortly thereafter, there was one morning when he didn't come down to breakfast because he was sick. Later, it became apparent that there was more going on.

"He was groaning something awful up there and he's pretty bad. So my mother went up. Someone said, 'You can't get in.' He'd locked the door. Someone wanted to break down the door, and she said 'No no no. We'll go…in the other apartment and go in that door.'"

So with the help of other boarders, Mrs. Roscoe went through another apartment to this man's room. Gertrude went on to explain what happened when she came home from school, understanding that something was very wrong. "I knew as soon as I opened the door. I could smell carbolic acid." But her mother was unsuccessful, and the man died.[156]

The Burnham's Falls, at Drake's Woods, was named after a resident, though in this case after another suicide. As a consequence of his business, one of the early forges in the Village, Orrin Burnham became depressed and jumped over the falls. It is this event that named the site.[157]

Uriah Arnold died in 1856, leaving a widow and seven children. As noted earlier, he was a carpenter and millwright, having built many of the forges in the county and in New York as well. He was crushed at a mill in Weybridge while making repairs to one of the forges that he had built. A large vat that he was transporting from one building to another rolled onto him when a heavy wind toppled him.

Another similar death by crushing took place in 1825. Samuel Plumley was digging iron ore for Wheeler and Bradbury, a local firm, along with Luther Graves. The ore bed collapsed, killing Plumley, while Graves was fortunate enough to barely escape.[158]

In the early years of electricity, from 1897 to 1912, Bristol's electricity was fed from a company in Rocky Dale. Mr. Tart lived next door to that operation, alongside the New Haven River. One winter, the high water rose behind ice dams, and when they broke, the water came down the river at such a furious pace that his little house was swept away. According to

Nellie Martin, who recalls that time, his body was later found downriver in Fuller's Flats.

FUNERAL PARLORS AND GRAVEYARDS

The first undertaker formed a business in Bristol in 1876. At that time, Mervin Varney hung out his shingle, adding J.J. Ridley as his partner in 1882. This was located on the south side of Main Street. Interestingly, both Varney and his first competitor, Smith Hatch, operated furniture stores. Hatch's funeral home was also located on Main Street's south side in what has since become known as the Hatch Block.

Hatch's son and successor, Ryland, took over the furniture store of both and sold his undertaking business to Varney in 1914, thus separating the businesses. Varney's son, Enoch, became an undertaker upon his own father's death. This funeral home was destroyed in the 1924 fire but moved

The Hatch Block. Smith Hatch operated a furniture store and a funeral home here. Other businesses have been located in the building, most recently No Knees Bar and today's popular pub, Dan's Place (2009).

to South Street—this location has remained an undertaking businesses. In 1961, the neighboring cinema, the Colonial Theatre, which had provided local entertainment since 1915, was purchased to enlarge the premises.

The first burial ground was located in Bristol Flats. This is where many notables and most of the population were buried until 1810. It is said to have been relocated, its graves moved at one time. They have not been found in the other cemeteries, so their locations remain a mystery.

A second graveyard, Greenwood Cemetery, has its earliest gravestones dating to 1802. Many early settlers were buried here—the Eastmans, Robert Dunshee and Robert and Manchester Holley, Araph Parmalee, George Sumner and Abraham Gaige, for example. It was not until 1895 that a record book was kept of the graves there, when Edwin Hasseltine began a log for the selectmen.

Other cemeteries include Briggs Hill Cemetery, a family graveyard named after Elisha Briggs, who owned considerable land there. This part of Bristol was later ceded to Lincoln. Meehan Cemetery was used primarily between 1802 and 1844. The first burial at Varney Cemetery, similarly established as a family site, was in 1809, with most of the other gravestones dating from 1840 to 1890.[159]

Mount Saint Joseph Catholic Cemetery was marked out in 1897 and is still in use. It is owned by the Burlington Catholic Diocese and located at the corner of Plank and Burpee Roads.

Part VIII

Sanctions, Myths and Rituals

Orcemus Shumway, a child of Deruses Shumway, about three years old, in the month of June 1806 wandered away [and was later found]... *The Writer was himself present on the occasion and well remembers the good feeling manifested, and smiling countenances of all who participated in the Search.*

–Honorable Harvey Munsill, Esq.[160]

VALUES

This is not a story about a boy's disappearance so much as that of the nature of community, the joining of a considerable number of people in the task of finding the lost child of one of their number.

First, the family searched for the boy, who was believed to have been lost while heading on a track or road going northward from the top of Stony Hill—perhaps where Airport Road or Liberty Street now run. They searched through the night but he wasn't found, and word had spread about his being missing, so the residents of both Bristol and neighboring towns mounted a search. This four- or five-hour search was followed by another, still more people from adjoining towns taking part. After another three hours' search of new ground, the boy was found sitting at the base of a pine tree.

The values of small-town living remain strong in Bristol and are based on the same things that kept Harvey Munsill's colleagues working together for the sake of the community writ large. It's the kindness of face-to-face interaction, whether you know the person or not, the value of seeing other people as essentially good and part of the community.

Benefit concerts and dances are held to raise money for the medical needs of both children and adults in specific and extreme circumstances, and country store counters commonly have a jar for the same purpose in

Pre-1950s postcard of North Street. *Courtesy of George Vince.*

South Mountain dominates the village's scenic beauty (1950s?). *Courtesy of George Vince.*

which shoppers donate their change. The flooding in August 2004 was followed by such a benefit to help those whose homes were damaged, including a local midwife's.

Winfred Trudo's story shows the interrelatedness of community connection. Trudo, the son of an orphan, wasn't sure where or when his family came to Bristol, but he grew up here. Trudo's father had been orphaned at age five and brought up in New Haven. But Josie Pecor believed that there was a Lincoln connection: Trudo's grandfather had perhaps originally come from that town. She was certain that he had never lived in the Notch. Josie had this as a matter of recall, as she was growing up in the Village at the time and would have known of the Trudo family, who were closely connected socially.

She had, for example, shopped at the store run by Trudo's grandfather. She was good friends with a boy named Rupert who clerked there. When the shopkeeper had a broken leg, having been kicked by his horse, Josie and another girl from church visited him.

At thirteen years old, Josie also witnessed Win's parents' courtship. The Jacobs, Win's mother's family, lived next door on Spring Street. The young couple spent evenings sitting out on the veranda, while this nosey neighbor watched. Win was born two years later. Josie was friendly with the Jacobs sisters, Laura and Blanche, and a brother, Jim, dated her older sister; Trudo also remembered playing with Josie's brother, Otto.[161]

Mountain Street in the 1950s. *Courtesy of George Vince.*

These values reach across class and social boundaries. Dr. Bosworth was connected with the Mary Fletcher Hospital, where he operated on Joann Kilbourn, Alan's "Lame Grandma," when she had a leg injury. He brought her home in the private plane that took him to and from the village. They were "going the same way," as it were. That it may seem unlikely to city-dwellers is because of the anonymity of urban life.

Among those listed by Munsill as Bristol's overseers of the poor included Soloman Drake, Harvey Munsill, Luman Munson and Datus R. Gaige. It was the duty of the community to look after its own.

In this way, there is a sense that Sam McKinnon belonged to everybody in town. This comes, I think, not just from Sam being a gregarious man and living a very public life at the service station, but also from his childhood experience. Sam and his twin, Alice, were raised by different grandmothers after the death of their mother. The affection with which people speak of this history showed a sense that without a mother it was partly up to the entire community to bring up these children. It's the same tone of voice heard in Josie Pecor's interview with Win Trudo and her searching her memory for information for him. She provided him with what details she could of where Trudo's father belonged in the local story because he had no family to impart that heritage. It was important to her to give him knowledge of his place in the community through family.

Third-grade students and their teacher. Sam McKinnon is bottom left; his twin sister Alice is the girl farthest right in the next row back (1918).

Other such core rural values include generosity and hospitality. They are shown a great deal in Bristol, which has not seemed to allow the cynicism of the wider world to seep in.

Sam McKinnon was known to be a particularly parsimonious man, yet also very generous. One of his favorite tales, known by nearly everyone in town, was of the honeymoon couple with the car that he was shocked to see run at all. "How did you ever get here with this car like this?" he asked. The young man had apparently just nursed it along. He insisted that whatever Sam did he not put in new spark plugs.

Sam sent the couple off for a meal and examined the car. Of course the car needed new spark plugs. It was in such bad shape that Sam put in some other parts, too, but told the young man that he had merely cleaned the spark plugs.

"I lied to him," Sam said. And when the customer asked how much he owed, Sam said he took a blank piece of paper, wrote on it "This is your wedding present—have a good time" and gave it to the man, who turned it over and asked, "What's this?" Sam replied, "Just what it says."

"You can't afford to do this," he protested, but Sam assured him that he could. "Things were going good for me," Sam explained to the interviewer.

SANCTIONS

The kinds of sanctions for misbehavior and crime that we recognize today are not altogether different from those of the past, but fines cited by Harvey Munsill, from an era before his own, struck him as being worth noting. There were other laws, however, which today seem rather strange.

The original charter for Pocock states that all the white pine and other pine trees that were suitable for masts for the Royal Navy were not to be cut without a special license, no matter whose land they were located on. If such trees were harvested without the license, the perpetrator's property would be forfeited for eternity, and he would also be penalized by confinement or fine.

That wasn't all. The original charter also demanded that five acres of land be cultivated for five years for every fifty acres that a landowner held. Also, each settler was enjoined to improve and settle according to other rules, also on penalty of losing the land. These laws resembled those made later for the homesteaders in the western territories.

Munsill's history records no violations of these statutes, nor have I pursued the question. Legal sanctions are often the least interesting topics to social historians and their audiences. More compelling are the informal ones. This is what people mean when they say that living in small towns like Bristol is "like living in a fish bowl." Our sanctions are sometimes very personal.

Munsill records this conventional crime occurring in 1806: "Joshua Henshaw…had a Store of goods in Bristol…and the Store was entered by some person unknown in the Night and robbed of a large portion of the most valuable part of the dry goods."

However, it had a bizarre, small country town kind of outcome. Circumstantial evidence pointed to Joshua Buffam as the culprit, and he was arrested and brought before Robert Holley, "where a court of enquiry was had." There was, in the end, insufficient evidence to hold and try him. However, before this became apparent, "[I]t was whispered to Buffam that if he could have his goods the matter would be dropped, otherwise he would most likely be bound over."

Buffam protested his innocence yet again but offered his conjecture that it was most likely that whoever did do the crime had probably hidden the goods nearby. He then "enquired if search had been made in a small piece of Wet ground about sixty rods West of the Store, on the South side of the road, and near the point of a ledge on the North side," saying that this particular location would be a likely hiding place and a good place for the authorities to look. They did, found the stolen goods and returned them to Henshaw. The story continues that, essentially, the town turned a blind eye to Buffam.[162]

This is the kind of sanction described here. People are aware of them at some level. That's a social sanction, critical to the endurance of relationships in small-town living.

As noted in the preface, even those who are sixth-generation Bristol people do not know everyone in town, but rather they know *of* one another. This is how: reputation and social sanctions reveal the limits of acceptable behavior where and when citizens rely on one another and live in proximity. It's an intimate lifestyle that can be disrupted by someone breaking the social or structural rules, not just the laws.

Yet nonconformity is accepted too. Gussie and Juna, in their later years, regularly rode their rider lawnmower in the Village. Characters like them and like Sam are embraced in small towns like Bristol where both independence and interdependence are valued. It is a gift to those of us from away to enjoy them.

Sam McKinnon is a man with a wonderful reputation in Bristol. "Everyone" remembers Sam and his filling station. One story about Sam shows the boundaries that even a man held in such high esteem comes up against in a small community.

This was recounted by one of the Old Farts, a mail carrier at the time. One day, when he brought along the mail, Sam mentioned that he had to get a haircut but didn't have the cash for it. The mailman was given a $100 bill and asked to get some change. The mail delivered, the postman went to the bank, got the change and took it back to Sam. He concluded, "He was just like that, he trusted people." Then, after a pause he added, "Not everybody," without further comment. A moment still later came the reflection, "He was good at keeping track of who owed him money. If you charged your gas… He had a great memory. He wrote what you owed him on his hand."

Many of the recollections of Sam as a businessman show him to be a classic Yankee, sure of himself and intolerant of others telling him what to do. The story concerns an Internal Revenue Service official who came to watch how Sam operated his business. The story goes that at the end of the day, the IRS man came to Sam and said, "Mr McKinnon, you never went to the register with any of that cash." To which Sam said, "Where's it say I have to?"

Having a reputation for all the right values and for treating people with fairness or generosity is what people expect and hope for, but some of Bristol's prominent citizens have not always enjoyed that. Here is a contrasting example. Though not from the same era, the comparison is revealing because it has to do with the value of money, the nature of generosity and the boundaries of acceptance.

Where there is a hint that Sam McKinnon might have been overly conscious about money and how much he was owed, such stories are tempered by great respect and affection for the man. On the other hand, Dr. Wright, the veterinarian, had an altogether different reputation.

Gussie Levarn told of a time when he had accidentally run over a local cat with his car and immediately took it into his office to see to it. The cat was beyond saving yet the owner was charged for Dr. Wright's services, including putting the cat down, despite the doctor being responsible for the injuries.

Similarly, it is said that when Dr. Wright invited someone to a meal out, it was, in fact, to a fast-food chain, rather than to the expected sit-down meal in a restaurant. "He was terribly tight. You could write a book!" There was no tempering of the negative with a warm or admiring comment or tale, except that his wife, Leah, "was a sweetheart."[163]

MYTHS AND RITUALS

Myths and mysteries do not abound in Bristol; it's a pretty straightforward place. The few stories are well-known. The most famous, a story of lost treasure, had been recounted in previous histories and in Joe Citro's *Green Mountains, Dark Tales*. As Citro notes, it is a common story in rural mountain towns, but he offers some basis for the validity of at least the initial story.

About 1800, a Spaniard named DeGrau was found digging in an area at the base of South Mountain, now known as "the Money Diggings." He claimed to be looking for a stash of silver that had been hidden in a cave by his father and his colleagues when DeGrau was a boy. The men left, carrying with them as much as they could, but no one had returned since. Citro speculates that there was reason for believing that something valuable had been buried there, if not silver ingots. DeGrau spent considerable time and energy excavating.

Between the time of DeGrau and 1889, a Canadian expedition began selling shares in the treasure for investors. At the time, *Bristol Herald* journalist Franklin Harvey took this to be an honest, if ill-fated, undertaking rather than a scam.[164]

Over the centuries, treasure seekers have come and gone, and the story still lives and the site remains a curiosity today.

The Lord's Prayer Rock (1910). *Courtesy of the Bristol Historical Society.*

Another tale is rather less far-fetched for some, if not for others. The Lord's Prayer Rock is a prominent landmark on the road toward the east, on the south side of Routes 17 and 116. The Protestant version of the Christian Lord's Prayer is engraved onto its surface, facing the road, and its corner is painted white to alert motorists to it, as it lies quite close to the pavement.

Its story is recorded by the granddaughter of the man said to have had it engraved there:

> *When Joseph C. Greene was a boy and lived in South Starksboro, one of his tasks was to take the logs from the mountain top to the sawmill in Bristol. The 9 Bridge Road, or Drake Woods Road, in those days was a terrific ride. Not only were there nine bridges to cross, but the logs were big and apt to slide off. When he arrived at the "Big Rock," he knew his problems were over, so he said a little prayer and breathed a sign of relief knowing he would once more get his logs to the mill safely.*
>
> *Years later, when he was a practicing physician in Buffalo, New York...* [he] *decided to come home and have the Lord's Prayer chiseled on the rock that had given him peace of mind and a feeling of security when he was a boy.*[165]

This conflicts somewhat with another, more colorful, story of the rock cited by the contributor of the "Prayer Rock Letterbox" information on the Internet:

> *One of the old stories about this rock is in the early days of the town when the loggers would haul their logs into town they had to climb a steep hill and would cuss and swear at their teams of horses to get them to get a good head of speed to make the climb. As the story goes, a Christian man who was well to do decided to have the prayer carved into the rock to help remind the drivers to keep their tongues in check.*[166]

The Bristol Lord's Prayer Rock letterbox was the first letterbox in the United States.

NICKNAMES

Here is a quiz for those living or visiting in Bristol today. Many of those who are famous or infamous within the town had nicknames, some of clear origin and some more obscure. Who knows the real names of these Bristol residents of times past? There are others, many others, throughout

Arthur W. "Dude" Prince as a young man. He was born in 1876 and celebrated his eightieth with the entire town in Holley Hall. *Courtesy of the Bristol Historical Society.*

the town, regulars whom everybody knows. I mention a few here as a sampling only. I wonder what this convention means about a town like Bristol; does it happen everywhere?

The story of how Sam McKinnon got his name is well-known in town. He was born Alan P. McKinnon in 1908 but was "Sam" by the age of six. As he tells it, Sam walked into one of the downtown shops, and "They were talking about 'the war [World War I]'" and commenting about the recruitment poster on the wall showing Uncle Sam pointing out to the viewer. One of the men in the conversation said, "Here comes Uncle Sam now" as the boy walked in and, as Sam put it, "the name stuck."[167]

Another famous town personality known primarily by his nickname was the aforementioned Dude Prince (see part two). He was born Arthur W. Prince in 1876 to parents living in Bristol. Cemetery records give no clue as to who his parents were or how they came to town. No one can say how he got the moniker. Perhaps, because of his Bristol Inn uniform, the formal livery including top hat, he transformed into something of a dude. No doubt someone in town knows the story.

Prince drove the Bristol Inn's horse-drawn coach from the railroad depot on North Street. Old photographs show him attired in a uniform while driving the coach. After the railroad stopped running, Prince wound the town clock up in the tower of Holley Hall once weekly for twenty-five years and worked at other odd jobs around the town. Young men, like musician/carpenter Fran Robideau, continue to make a living in Bristol this way.

On his eightieth birthday, there was a town-wide celebration at Holley Hall to honor Prince. About two hundred townspeople came. He lived another six years, dying in 1962. At some point in time, perhaps when 911 addresses were initiated in the 1990s, Prince Lane was named for him.

Another man known for his attention to his appearance was called Acey. Acey Jackman was said to be quite a handsome man, tall and well dressed. The story goes that his mother made sure he dressed well as he was growing up and that he became known for this by his schoolmates. As an adult, he was a popular physical education teacher at the high school. Acey, whose given name was Kenneth, was of the well-known Jackman family, a younger brother of Glenn and uncle to Fred, of Jackmans, Inc. It was for this pristine and stylish appearance that he was known from boyhood as Acey.[168]

Gussie's husband, Leonard Leroy Levarn, was known as Rosie. He acquired the moniker as a child, for his rosie cheeks. And Gussie? Her given name was Christine Bostwick.

One big purchase for Royal Peake was, as mentioned in part three, his car, the first in town. Peveril Peake's diary quotations include "R.W. Peake's locomobile came to Bristol." Peveril told of "showing off the car" at the county fair that was held in Middlebury at the time. The car was locally manufactured and bought from a Burlington man, who had been the first in Vermont to have a car. It ran on steam and took two days for Rollie to get it to Bristol. It was his pride and joy.

"They wanted him to run around the track to show it but people…bet…[on the] horses and ran races so by the time it was his turn, he'd run out of steam half way around. Everyone," as Peveril related the story, "turned their backs and went on to do other things. That was the last time my father displayed it."

When Rollie's father died, the funeral director "implored" Rollie to leave the car at home and hire a trap so that the car wouldn't scare the horses drawing the hearse.[169]

A recent publication by Lincoln writer Chris Bohjalian tells of a nearly unknown Bristol man whose story isn't one of prosperity but rather reveals how, as Bohjalian put it, "a person can wind up homeless, despite friends or family, talent or brains."

Bob Campbell had been a spectacular photographer of musical celebrities and visual chronicler of the social changes taking place in the 1960s and '70s. Campbell grew up in Bristol, coming into the village as a ten-year-old, to be cared for by an aunt and uncle, Elizabeth and Daniel Borzone. He had worked in theatre in New York and spent time in California but found himself at a homeless shelter in Burlington in the mid-1990s. Nonetheless, he felt a strong connection to Bristol, returning often to collect water from a spring near the Village to bring back to his apartment in Burlington. He was apparently brilliant and eccentric but weakened by a stroke that he'd had in the 1980s, leaving him unable to work professionally. Another stroke killed him in February 2002.

Bohjalian retells three schoolmates' memories of him in his article. Ruth Tromley, Shirley Purinton-Ahlberg and Dorothy Dalton-Fleming knew nothing of his photographic career but remembered him as enjoying music, being the only boy who could dance. Purinton-Ahlberg called him a "walking dictionary. He read the *New York Times* every day, even in sixth grade."

Campbell's nickname, given by the other children at school, reflects affection. It refers, of course, to "the red cans in their parents' pantries, and not because he had a special fondness for soup."[170]

Part IX

From Away: Incomers, Locals and Travelers

Our train is whistling in, hear the echoes come back,
From the Rockey range at the end of the track,
Welcome home by the mountainside
After a tiresome railway ride?
To a stranger it would almost appear,
That many trains were drawing near
Bristol is truly a lovely spot,
For any purpose I care not what.
–*Willis Peake, as quoted in Peveril Peake's "Peake Family Collection"*[171]

TOURISTS, TRAVELERS AND VISITORS

People have come to Bristol to convene with others of similar interests, some to learn and some for social events.

During annual encampments of social organizations like the Vermont Division of the Society of Veterans, the Ladies Aid Society and the Addison County Baptist Association, all held in the summer of 1900, participants stayed at the Bristol House, where some of the events were held. When Holley Hall was built, it had a seating capacity of five hundred, which suited this kind of large gathering and made such opportunities available to the growing town.

In the 1930s and '40s, Bristol housed Middlebury College's German School, providing the hallmark of its programs—a certain isolation so that students can become immersed in the language of study. Students gathered here in this small rural community to do nothing but live and speak with other students and their teachers.

Bristol was a tourist destination as soon as its beauty and prosperity were marketed (1907). *Courtesy of Thomas Wells.*

Today, the national headquarters for Phoenix Rising Yoga Therapy on Mountain Street brings people from all over the country and even abroad to participate in its training programs. The wonderful setting that Munsill wrote about two hundred years ago is still an incentive for such visitors. They contribute to Bristol's economy by visiting restaurants and shops, as they always have.

One of Vermont's oldest industries, though not often touted, is that of entertaining tourists. Today, it is big business in Vermont, but it has been so for quite some time. In his history, Munsill noted the beauty of Bristol and the surrounding scenery. There have always been people seeking refuge in such a calm and beautiful place.

In 1900, visitors coming to enjoy Bristol's scenery and to hike and climb local hills was common enough for a resort to be considered realistic by Joseph Battell of Middlebury. At that time, he opened "a favorite resort for tourists and mountain climbers…Mr. Battell has erected a lodge, called 'Battell Lodge' about 100 rods from the summit [of a nearby mountain], a sort of half way house so constructed that small parties can stop there overnight."

Bristol has continued to rely on such visitors' contribution to the local economy through a variety of means. Through the years, celebrations of local history have been a means of doing this. The Fourth of July Independence Parade draws people every year, as do the weekly Bristol Band concerts.

"Greetings from Bristol, Vermont." Bristol was still considered a tourist spot (1950s). *Courtesy of Thomas Wells.*

In 1912, during Old Home Week, a town pageant was held with a parade of floats depicting the founders and other historic events. In the same way, the 2009 Previously Pocock Street Fair commemorated local history and encouraged visitors to come to the town.

At one point, the Bristol House and the Commercial House both provided lodging for tourists and other visitors, on either end and opposite sides of Main Street. The Bristol House was first operated as a public house by Robert Holley and grew into a hotel later, in 1820, with Abram Gaige as its landlord. Over the decades, the building changed hands and ambience.

Later called the Bristol Inn, it was a famous landmark in town until it was demolished in 1961. Before that, there had been public houses and taverns at which visitors might spend the night. The O'Neill Block itself had a hotel at one time, before it became a storefront. During the period from 1871 through 1896, J.J. Ridley was proprietor. Transportation was provided to and from the railroad depot in New Haven.

Its customers were primarily men. Traveling salesmen made their base there, hiring a horse and buggy from a local stable to take them to their customers throughout the neighboring towns. The Bristol House was also a meeting place for men to discuss the happenings of the day because it was also the weekly distribution point for the mail delivery in town. Still others were boarders in the town.

A Founders' Day Pageant during Old Home Week. It included a parade of floats depicting the founders and other historic events (1912). *Courtesy of the UVM Landscape Change Program and the Bristol Historical Society.*

The Bristol House became a more chic establishment under the ownership of the Burnhams (1913). *Courtesy of the UVM Landscape Change Program and the Bristol Historical Society.*

The Bristol House coach and mules. During the building's life as the Bristol House, passengers were escorted from the train station (1900–1906). *Courtesy of the UVM Landscape Change Program and the Bristol Historical Society.*

This would have been a particularly good place for traveling businessmen to stay because it *was* the place where tradesmen and decision makers in town gathered. Here they would meet and talk with these prominent citizens, which could only be good for business.

The first competition for the Bristol House came at the other end of town. The Commercial House was opened in the 1880s by Ryland Hatch. There was also a livery stable located there.

Mrs. Roscoe's boardinghouse also catered to visitors here for work or pleasure, including Bristol resident and future dentist Bill Cardell. When he first left dental school, Cardell and his wife brought other couples to join them in Bristol every summer. At the boardinghouse, Mrs. Roscoe would bring out the fancy linen tablecloths and napkins for them.

The picture of the small rural village isolated in its bucolic surroundings is popular among those from away, and sometimes it is encouraged by locals, but Bristol has never been such an isolated place, even from its earliest days. People have passed through and often stayed because of all the variety of reasons people do such things—for work, to follow or join family, because of opportunities of affordable land and housing and so on. The advent of

Joseph W. "Joe" Rock came to Bristol to run the Bristol Airport, constructed under the Works Progress Administration in combination with town funds. He died in a plane crash in 1960, and the airport was sold to the district in 1966; it is now the home of Mount Abraham Union High School (late 1930s).

the automobile and the brief life of the local airport merely increased the comings and goings of people from away.

THE JOURNEY HOME: HOW FAMILIES CAME TO BRISTOL

There was a great movement of the population in postwar America—after the Revolutionary War, that is. Several of the men who settled their families here in the early years were veterans of that conflict. Samuel Stewart, the Eastmans, Captain Gurdon Munsill and Robert Holley were among them, arriving shortly after Pocock had been chartered and organized as a town.

Bristol, like so many other nearby towns, was the stopping place of veterans of the Civil War also, seeking the same thing: to start a family and a new chapter of their lives.

We have a tendency to think, to believe, that those families whose names have been part of Bristol's story for generations were destined to be here, that they made the one move from somewhere to Bristol and became its backbone. Our picture of history is that people just didn't move around much. But just like us, people and families *did* move from place to place, following the availability of good farmland or its reasonable price, following job prospects, joining family or pursuing opportunity. When they found it, they stayed. Some of the next generation moved away; others stayed, pretty much as we do today.

The Peake family is a good example of the kind of settlers who came to Bristol after it was somewhat established but was not yet the vibrant economic center that it later became. Seth Peake was born in 1784 in New York State and had quite a journey of stops and starts in his migration from Nantucket to Bristol, beginning with his parents' flight from persecution from Nantucket Island.

"They left Nantucket," Peveril Peake began the story. "The English took over the island and quartered troops there [in the Revolutionary War]" and harassed the Quakers, among which were the Peake family. One incident caused the family to decide that it was time to leave.

As Peveril tells it, "William Peake had a store. A molasses barrel was overturned [as part of the harassment], so he traded it for a sloop. They went down through New York harbor to Cohoes, New York, where they traded the sloop for oxen and a cart." Thereafter they made their way north and lived near Hebron, New York, for a few years, where they clearly planned to settle because they joined the Society of Friends there. However, they ventured into Vermont, living first in Ferrisburgh and later in Monkton, where William died.

Son Seth, from which Peveril Peake's family descended, moved from Monkton to Bristol, where he was a merchant and lender and became a leader in the town, his saddle shop being located on South Street, approximately where the funeral home now stands. The shop was directly across the street from where the Holley family lived; they soon became related on the marriage of Jane Holley to Seth's son, Royal.

Just as we often complain that taxes are just getting too high and out of control, Royal said the same in the mid-1880s. So he packed up to live elsewhere. He moved to New York City and was back in six months. The big city, apparently, wasn't the life that suited him. Perhaps he missed his connection to a community who knew him and his family well. Anyway, high taxes couldn't keep him away, and he remained part of Bristol's heritage. The story is that he invested in land in the west and increased the size of his own holding, known as "the Royal Peake farm" well into the 1900s.[172]

The family history of Josie Pecor well reflects the process by which the town has become populated through the years and that brings people to Bristol still. Her people on her father's side, the Monroes, came from Sutton, Quebec. Several families came together, she recalled in a taped interview, when her father was about nine years old. They brought along their own parents, making three generations of Monroes to come, and one of Josie's grandmother's brother, who eventually moved down to Forest Dale, Vermont.

The Monroes first moved into the Notch in 1858, moving later into the Flats. By the time the telephone company was installed at her father's house, Josie was in her teens. She later married Vernon Pecor. By then, the family was well entrenched in village life.

People coming from away, both to visit and live, have been a part of Bristol's story for a long time. They include, as we have mentioned, French Canadians coming in from Canada and a number of Irish in the later 1800s, having fled the famine in their own country. In the 1970s, hippies came north to Vermont, including Bristol, to escape the conventional suburban life in which they had grown up during the postwar years. They came in a movement "back to the land" to raise their families surrounded by nature and in face-to-face relationships with neighbors. One of these hippies became a prosperous local businessman, Kevin Harper, whose small factory that began by manufacturing natural baby products now provides lip balm to an international market, under new ownership.

Everyone came here from somewhere else—people moving in search of better resources or jobs, or following family. Such movement adds diversity and keeps the community vibrant. Those for whom it is a true fit stay here, absorbing the culture of this particular small town and adding a new chapter as well. Others move on.

Part X

My People, My Village, My Home

Several persons that had formerly lived in Bristol that have died, and been brought back to Bristol to be buried.

–Honorable Harvey Munsill, Esq.[173]

Since the earliest days, people who had lived in Bristol but died elsewhere have been buried in one of Bristol's graveyards. The earliest of these were Henry and Mary McLaughlin, whose story was related in part two and whose son, Thadeus, stayed to become postmaster. Also buried there, in 1858, was the Honorable Samuel W. Holley, the son of the early settler Robert. His widow was buried beside him years later.

Among Bristol's forbears were those who made their names and fortunes elsewhere. At least one returned to Bristol or Vermont to be buried. This was Ezra Butler (E.B.) Eddy, whose factory in Hull, Quebec—the French-speaking sister city to Ottawa—manufactured friction matches. Though born in Bristol in 1827, Eddy is remembered in Brattleboro as a tin peddler.

Eddy was the son of Samuel Eddy, one-time proprietor of the Bristol House, and his wife, an Eastman girl, Clarissa. Eddy began his career in Quebec making wooden matches from discarded wood products from sawmills. He expanded his factory and manufactured other wooden products, rebuilding after a fire in that city in 1882 and expanding into a pulp and paper company. A second fire in 1900 did not deter him, and he rebuilt yet again. He is known in Canada as a major employer and political figure of his era, and the Eddy Match Company is still a prospering business as of this writing.[174]

For many from away residents, quite the opposite has been true: rather than being buried in family plots in faraway states, many "flatlanders" have literally put down roots in Bristol. This was true from the first migration. An Eastman or Eddy considered himself a native of Bristol; this was his home.

CONTROVERSY

Over the years there have been controversies and disagreements about how the town should be governed or over the use of resources, business planning, development and other things, as in all places.

One fairly recent controversy changed Bristol in a way that has had important consequences for both town and village. That was when the two merged as one in 1994, known locally as "the Merger." George Smith, who operates the landfill on Pine Street, sat on the board of selectmen at the time. He regrets that he encouraged that change, explaining that he felt at the time that the merger would reduce the expenses of the citizens of Bristol for a variety of services. When interviewed later, he felt that that proved not to be the case.[175]

Differing values within the community are manifested without direct, socially disruptive, conflict. Since late 2002, before the country engaged in the second war with Iraq and toppled Saddam Hussein, there has been a Friday evening peace vigil held on the corner of the green at North and Main Streets. A regular group of citizens meets at 5:00 p.m. and has a quiet protest against the war, complete with signs and slogans, standing in front of the cannon that has stood at that corner since the Civil War. For a while, there was a similar set of citizens across the street, a group whose signs showed that they supported the troops and, consequently, the war.

Another contemporary controversy has been over the application for a zoning permit by Jim Lathrop for an approximately thirty-acre gravel pit about a mile from the downtown. Jim's great-great-grandfather was Noah Lathrop. His brother, Tom Lathrop, runs Lathrop's Maple Supply, specializing in sustainable forestry and locally harvested wood products. In the fall of 2008, the proposal was rejected by the Bristol Zoning Board.

The pit project had been vocally opposed by well-known figures in the downtown business community—this generation's Cypran, Oliver and Jonathan Eastman, Harvey Munsill, Noble Dunshee, A.B. Kilbourn and Dr. Bosworth. This time, many of these players are from away, "flatlanders" who have come to Bristol to enjoy what it has to offer in contrast to the cities from which they have often come.

It is characteristic of small towns that those who consider themselves true locals rely on those from away to be involved in just this kind of public debate, while keeping in the background themselves—less vocal if not less firm in their views, as noted in the preface. The Lathrops believed that their supporters outnumbered the opponents but that those in favor of the pit were somehow powerless and/or just not speaking up by attending hearings.

One newspaper reported that George Smith believed that "the majority of people opposed to the pit aren't Bristol natives." He characterized the opponents this way: "There's only a few people holding it up, but they're doing it legally, so we can't do anything."[176]

The closest neighbor is similarly a Bristol native who was, in fact, vocal in opposition to the proposal, as was his mother. Greg Moye's family has lived in Bristol since the 1800s, like the Lathrops, his great-grandfather having worked at the Lathrop mill. He and his mother, Michelle, feel that the modern mill itself has been detrimental to the New Haven River along which it sits and that the gravel pit would similarly damage the landscape. Theirs is a case of local opposition to another local's initiative. The local versus from away juxtaposition is a common way for communities with a generous mix of both to minimize internal strife. It is a means by which the conflict is mitigated, by infusing it with the idea that the disagreement was generated from without rather than within. It is useful in preventing long-term divisions within communities.

The recent past shows how, despite deep discord about a single topic, Bristol people support their views without opening engaging in hostility and dividing the community. This is a small-town New England way and must have been similarly present in the past to maintain the peace within while giving voice to differing views. No one knows, for example, why (only when) the village of Pocock became Bristol; the story was lost even in the 1860s, when Harvey Munsill penned his papers. It may have been by consensus, it may have been by controversy, but who knows. And the choice of a new name? There may have been fiercely contentious debates. But the quiet, hidden nature of such rifts in small towns allows them to maintain a cohesive view of themselves at the time and, more importantly, in the future. It helps to maintain the ethic of "my people, my village, my home" for everyone.

THE FUTURE RETURNS TO THE PAST

The history of a town is "gathered from little things, many of which are never recorded, yet they are full of interest and when obtained, [provide] a rich inheritance, and constitute a valuable legacy to be bequeathed to those yet unborn."[177]

These little things, which go unrecorded, are the lives of everyday people, and when people are living these little things, it does not occur to them to record them. Our notion of history is of the past, but of course every day we are making future generations' history. We are so very fortunate that the experiences of Bristol residents began to be recorded in the late 1970s by the Bristol Historical Society and by the Vermont Folklife Center in Middlebury, as they continue to be.

As the present gradually becomes the past, those little things get lost. This is a process that is hardly visible to us. Only a few years ago, one shop, Deerleap Books, stood on the spot originally known as Haymarket Square. It seems to be long forgotten that trade and events took place in this open space.

The first building there became Patnode's garage, whose outbuildings remain behind 25 Main Street. That original building has been modified a great deal in the last fifty years, and one of those iterations was the bookstore. Already there are probably residents who never knew it was there. The building itself is now called the Deerleap Building, as the owners are Carol and Thomas Wells, the bookstore owners who later subdivided it to house three storefronts and several offices.

One of the very small things that has changed our orientation along this stretch of Main Street, as the years pass, is the location of the sidewalk. Before Deerleap Books closed, the sidewalk was moved from directly in front of it to the front of the National Bank of Middlebury, just yards farther east. During the first few years of this change, as the paint on the former sidewalk slowly deteriorated, it informally continued to be recognized as the place people cross the street.

Lately, however, now that those markings are mostly gone, the shift has been made and people not jaywalking now cross at this newer location. This may be because when BECKS Alley Antiques was restored after its 2007 fire, its front door was opened up again onto Main Street. For decades, it had only been accessible by the side door. The Thomas Building and Design Company, also the landlord, restored it in 2008 with access once again directly on the street. The new crosswalk begins just below its stoop. People regularly cross from the front door of the bank now to go right into the shop. Subtle, but a slight change in orientation that comes from a small change in how the town or state marks out the street and the placement of a doorway can make real differences over time.

The site of the National Bank of Middlebury has an interesting story, as well. It stands where Sam McKinnon's service station stood and became a used care dealership, Mad River Auto, in the 1980s. When the bank branch was established, the old building was razed. But it is interesting in the life of such a town as Bristol that Theresa Gile, the manager of the branch—whose office lies somewhere near where Sam's gas pumps must have stood—is Sam's great-niece through marriage. Her children knew Sam McKinnon as Uncle Sam. Before that, it was the site of the O'Neill Block, which fire destroyed in 1929. The newspapers of the day called it a landmark.

This is what I mean when I say "the future returns to the past." However the future revisits modern Bristol, just how the process works is a mystery because it happens right under our noses as we live every single day in the patterns of our behavior. What people knew and used and where they lived take on new functions and new names. And if these things that they knew don't continue to mean the same thing or have the same use, they are nonetheless still engaged in the ongoing life of the town—even after they are gone, like the O'Neill building and Noble Dunshee's house.

The older National Bank building located on the south side of Main Street now houses two law offices, and the upper story—with the marvelous, arched window—is the Walkover Gallery. Private and public events and art shows are held there. The old safe at the rear of the first floor, rather than be removed, is now used as a library and gallery, its door standing open to visitors' view. When it was renovated, the lobby floor was painted in a motif that replicates the gear work on the interior of the safe door.

Old buildings continue to be restored, sometimes renamed, change to new uses or reverted to old ones. The former Bristol Railroad Station is a perfect example of a creative change, a way to maintain a landmark without it becoming obsolete. It is now a private home.

Possibly the oldest building in town now houses the aforementioned antique shop. The next building to the east, the Hatch Block, is not known by that name. As noted in previous chapters, it has also been a hotel, a furniture store, a funeral parlor and shoe shop. In terms of orientation, it has been located on the outskirts of Main Street, something that might change with the recent opening of Dan's Place, a new and very popular tavern-style bar.

When purchased by a local consortium of business owners several years ago, the Dunshee Block, where Kimball's Office Services and Bristol Cliff's Music fill the storefronts, returned to our vocabulary. The building was renovated and brought up to date, but the exterior is the same in fundamentals as when William E. Dunshee built it. So many of the other buildings have, for now, lost those associated names, except perhaps for the Tomasi and the old bank blocks, which have their names engraved in their façades.

Across the street, a new Snap's restaurant was opened in 2003, resurrecting both the name and the spirit of Snap Palmer's place. That restaurant had been located where the shop Greetings now stands. A replica was made of the old sign for the new Snap's, which was so named because of the great popularity of the owner and the style of the place.

The First National Bank vault, now used as a library, for the law firms of Karen Lueders and James Dumont or sometimes as an art gallery.

South side of Main Street after the fire. The building to the right houses Feather the Nest; Vermont Honeylights and Greetings are now in the building to the left (October 1924). *Courtesy of the UVM Landscape Change Program and the Bristol Historical Society.*

The south side of Main Street today (2009).

Cheri Rockwood brought back an old tradition when she opened a new Snaps in 2003.

The Bristol Depot as a private home in 2009. Bought at auction by Mitchell Eldin Lathrop when the railroad was closed, it is now the home of his grandson Alan and family.

Visitors in town on a Friday will notice Pat Palmer's horse-drawn recycling wagon and think about how quaint Bristol maintains this means of trash collection. As residents know, however, this was a new venture introduced by the town in the early 1990s to save money. It has now shifted to a private business owned and operated by Palmer, who raises the hardworking Percherons on his New Haven farm.

The Bristol Downtown Community Partnership, the body granted a downtown designation by the State of Vermont in 2006, surveyed town residents as part of its permitting process. One of the dominant sentiments that emerged from that study was that the people of Bristol have a deep commitment to the history of the town and wish to see its heritage continue to be honored and preserved in any future development of the town, both its outlying areas and the village center.

With the rising cost of gasoline in late 2008, residents increasingly chose to do less driving outside Bristol for their shopping and entertainment. This trend toward buying locally and defining one's personal orientation in Bristol can only be a good thing for the furthering of these ideals and our small-town values as the new century moves forward. Bristol is not now, nor has it ever fully been, a bedroom community, although many residents' jobs take them to the larger centers of Middlebury and Chittenden County. Rather, the attraction of this town—both among those from away and those from long-standing local families—springs from the fact that Bristol is its own town with its own cultural identity. Contributing to this has been my purpose in writing this book.

Notes

PREFACE

1. Munsill, *Early History*, 257.
2. Skiffington, "Noblesse Oblige," 265–77.

I. FOUNDING FAMILIES' LEGACIES

3. Munsill, *Early History*, 254.
4. Ibid., 65–66.
5. Ibid.
6. Ibid., 69.
7. Ibid., 79.
8. Ibid., 75.
9. Outlook Club, *History of Bristol, Vermont*, 3rd ed., 1.
10. Munsill, *Early History*, 59–61a.
11. Ibid., 63–64a.
12. Gertrude Lathrop, interview, 2007.

II. THE SOCIAL MIX

13. Munsill, *Early History*, 237.
14. Carleton, ed. *Genealogical and Family History*, 477.
15. Munsill, *Early History*, 189.
16. Ibid., 190.
17. Outlook Club of Bristol, *History of Bristol, Vermont*, 1st ed., 57.
18. Carleton, *Family History*, 478.

19. Bristol Land Records, volume 7, p. 120, quoted in Outlook Club, *History of Bristol, Vermont*, 3rd ed., 69.
20. Outlook Club, *History of Bristol, Vermont*, 3rd ed., 4; Heffernan, "The Evolution and Demise of Drake & Smith Company."
21. Carleton, *Family History*, 474.
22. Ibid., 489–90.
23. Smith, "History of the Town of Bristol," 404.
24. Peake, "Peake Family Collection."
25. Outlook Club, *History of Bristol, Vermont*, 3rd ed., 72.
26. Hanson, et al., "Bristol Houses," interview, July 15, 1999.
27. Cragen, interview, 2001.
28. Levarn, "Voices from Vermont," interview, 1994.
29. Smith, "History of the Town of Bristol," 411.
30. Levarn and Levarn, "Voices from Vermont," interview, 1994.
31. Lewis and Heffernan, "Little Ireland," interview, 2003.
32. Levarn, "Gussie Levarn Reflects," interview, 2005.
33. Carleton, *Family History*, 479.
34. Ibid., 485.
35. Smith, "History of the Town of Bristol," 411.
36. Levarn, "Gussie Levarn Reflects," interview, 2005.

III. Structural Core: Building a Town

37. Smith, "History of the Town of Bristol," 407–8.
38. Ibid.
39. Outlook Club, *History of Bristol, Vermont*, 3rd ed., 40.
40. Smith, "History of the Town of Bristol," 409.
41. Outlook Club, *History of Bristol, Vermont*, 3rd ed., 41.
42. Carleton, *Family History*, 489–90.
43. Munsill, *Early History*, 36–39.
44. Nellie Martin, interview, 2001.
45. Munsill, *Early History*, 256.
46. Lathrop, interview, 2007.
47. Smith, "History of the Town of Bristol," 411.
48. Pecor, interview, 2001.
49. Tyler and Smith, "Remembering Bristol," interview, 2007.
50. Outlook Club, *History of Bristol, Vermont*, 3rd ed., 45–46.
51. Peake, "Peake Family Collection."
52. Levarn, "Gussie Levarn Reflects," interview, 2005.

53. Munsill, *Early History*, 220.
54. Outlook Club, *History of Bristol, Vermont*, 3rd ed., 50.
55. Kilbourn, interview, December 12, 2008.
56. Selden, interview, 2001.
57. Outlook Club, *History of Bristol, Vermont*, 3rd ed., 50.
58. Munsill, *Early History*, 138.
59. Tyler, Smith and Heffernan, interview, 2003.
60. *Bristol News*, June 6, 1900.
61. Munsill, *Early History*, 242.
62. Ibid., 242.
63. Levarn, "Gussie Levarn Reflects," interview, 2005.
64. Smith, "History of the Town of Bristol," 415.
65. Ibid., 415.
66. Lathrop, interview, 2007.
67. Lewis and Heffernan, "Little Ireland," interview, 2003.
68. Tyler and Smith, "Remembering Bristol," interview, 2007.
69. McKinnon, "Survey," interview, 1998.
70. Weston, "History of Bristol Band," interview, 2007.
71. *Bristol News*, June 20, 1900.
72. Outlook Club, *History of Bristol, Vermont*, 3rd ed., 66–68.
73. *Bristol News*, June 20, 1900.
74. Outlook Club, *History of Bristol, Vermont*, 3rd ed., 84.
75. Carleton, *Family History*, 478.
76. Munsill, *Early History*, appendix.
77. Outlook Club, *History of Bristol, Vermont*, 3rd ed., 80–84.
78. Carleton, *Family History*, 478.
79. Ibid.
80. Ibid.
81. Outlook Club, *History of Bristol, Vermont*, 3rd ed., 84.
82. Ibid., 80–84.

IV. THE LIFE CYCLE OF A VILLAGE

83. Levarn, "Gussie Levarn Reflects," interview, 2005.
84. Ibid.
85. Tyler and Smith, "Remembering Bristol," interview, 2007.
86. Levarn, "Gussie Levarn Reflects," interview, 2005.
87. Tyler and Smith, "Remembering Bristol," interview, 2007.
88. Munsill, *Early History*, 41.

89. Ibid., 219.
90. Ibid., 220.
91. *Bristol News*, June 6, 1900.
92. Levarn, "Gussie Levarn Reflects," interview, 2005.
93. Tyler and Smith, "Remembering Bristol," interview, 2007.
94. Bingham, "Boarding House Living," interview, 2007.
95. Ibid.
96. Tyler and Smith, "Remembering Bristol," interview, 2007.
97. Levarn, "Gussie Levarn Reflects," interview, 2005.
98. Levarn and Levarn, "Voices from Vermont," interview, 1994.
99. Levarn, "Gussie Levarn Reflects," interview, 2005.
100. Ibid.
101. Tyler and Smith, "Remembering Bristol," interview, 2007.
102. McKinnon, "Survey," interview, 1998.
103. Atkins, "A Cornhusker/Vermonter."
104. *Bristol News*, May 23, 1900.
105. Ibid., June 6, 1900.
106. Weston, "History of Bristol Band," interview, 2007.
107. Outlook Club, *History of Bristol, Vermont*, 3rd ed., 40, 86–89.
108. Tyler and Smith, "Remembering Bristol," interview, 2007.
109. Outlook Club, *History of Bristol, Vermont*, 3rd ed., 89–90.
110. Selden, interview, 2001.
111. Martin, interview, 2001.
112. Ibid.
113. Lathrop, interview, 2007.
114. Levarn, "Gussie Levarn Reflects," interview, 2005.
115. Bingham, "Boarding House Living," interview, 2007.
116. Cragen, interview, 2001.
117. Selden, interview, 2001.
118. Tyler and Smith, "Remembering Bristol," interview, 2007.
119. Ibid.
120. Atkins, "A Cornhusker/Vermonter."
121. Darling, "Laurie (Desorda) Darling's memories"; Davignon, "Church Street Gang."

V. LAND USE TALES: MILK, MILLS AND WOOD

122. Eaton, "History of Bristol, Vermont."
123. Lathrop, interview, 2007.

124. Coffin, personal communication, 2009.
125. Selden, interview, 2001.
126. Lathrop, interview, 2007.
127. *Bristol News*.
128. Munsill, *Early History*, 256.
129. Martin, interview, 2001.

VI. BRISTOL WOMEN AT WORK

130. Munsill, *Early History*, 238.
131. Levarn, "Gussie Levarn Reflects," interview, 2005.
132. Tyler and Smith, "Remembering Bristol," interview, 2007.
133. Martin, interview, 2001.
134. Ibid.
135. Lewis and Heffernan, "Little Ireland," interview, 2003.
136. Levarn, "Gussie Levarn Reflects," interview, 2005.
137. Bingham, "Boarding House Living," interview, 2007.
138. Levarn, "Gussie Levarn Reflects," interview, 2005.
139. Martin, interview, 2001.
140. Coffin, personal communication, 2009.
141. Selden, interview, 2001.
142. Tyler and Smith, "Remembering Bristol," interview, 2007.
143. Ibid.

VII. FIRE, FLOODS, DISASTER AND DEATH

144. *Bristol News*, May 16, 1900.
145. Outlook Club, *History of Bristol, Vermont*, 3rd ed., 43–44.
146. *Bristol News*, May 16, 1900.
147. Selden, interview, 2001.
148. Outlook Club, *History of Bristol, Vermont*, 3rd ed., 6.
149. Ibid., 45.
150. Munsill, *Early History*, 167–70.
151. Swift, "Diseases, Mortality," 320–21.
152. Munsill, *Early History*, 97.
153. Levarn, "Gussie Levarn Reflects," interview, 2005.
154. Swift, "Diseases, Mortality," 320–21.
155. Munsill, *Early History*, 160–61.

156. Bingham, "Boarding House Living," interview, 2007.
157. Outlook Club, *History of Bristol, Vermont*, 3rd ed., 95.
158. Munsill, *Early History*, 160–61.
159. Ibid., 204–6.

VIII. SANCTIONS, MYTHS AND RITUALS

160. Ibid.
161. Pecor, interview, 2001.
162. Munsill, *Early History*, 165–66.
163. Levarn, "Gussie Levarn Reflects," interview, 2005.
164. Citro, *Green Mountains, Dark Tales*, 144–49.
165. Outlook Club, *History of Bristol, Vermont*, 3rd ed., 93–94.
166. Davis, "Prayer Rock Letterbox, Bristol, VT, USA."
167. McKinnon, "Survey," interview, 1998.
168. Tyler and Smith, "Remembering Bristol," interview, 2007.
169. Peake, interview, 2001.
170. Bohjalian "Bob's Story," *Burlington Free Press*, 2003.

IX. FROM AWAY: INCOMERS, LOCALS AND TRAVELERS

171. Peake, "Peake Family Collection."
172. Peake, interview, 2001.

X. MY PEOPLE, MY VILLAGE, MY HOME

173. Munsill, *Early History*, 206a.
174. "Ezra Butler Eddy," Wikipedia, the free encyclopedia.
175. Tyler and Smith, "Remembering Bristol," interview, 2007.
176. Ives, "Bristol Zoning Board," *Seven Days*, September 26, 2008.
177. Munsill, *Early History*, 116.

Bibliography

Atkins, Jim. "A Cornhusker/Vermonter." Your Stories—Bristol Memories. http://bristolmemories.moonfruit.com/#/your-stories/4529882798.

Bingham, Gertrude. "Boarding House Living in the 1930's & 1940's." Interview. 2007. Bristol Historical Society, accession number 2007.009.001, audiocassette.

Bohjalian, Chris. "Bob's Story: The Picture of Compassion: Photographer Found Happiness at Shelter Long After Secretly Storied Career." *Burlington Free Press*, 2003.

Bristol News. April–June 1900.

Carlton, Hiram, ed. *Genealogical and Family History of the State of Vermont*. New York: Lewis Publishing Company, 1903.

Citro, Joe. *Green Mountains, Dark Tales*. Hanover, NH: University Press of New England, 1999.

Coffin, Sylvia. Personal communication. March 23, 2009.

Cragen, Florence. Interview. 2001. Bristol Historical Society, accession number 2001.003.017 (side 1), audiocassette.

Darling, Laurie (Desorda). "Laurie (Desorda) Darling's memories." Your Stories—Bristol Memories. http://bristolmemories.moonfruit.com/#/your-stories/4529882798.

Davignon Patrick. "Church Street Gang." Your Stories—Bristol Memories. http://bristolmemories.moonfruit.com/#/your-stories/4529882798.

Davis, Erik. "Prayer Rock Letterbox Map & Clues." http://home.snu.edu/~dwilliam/letbox/Bristol.htm.

Eaton, Cindy. "History of Bristol, Vermont, and the Industries that Shaped the Town." Unpublished paper, Community College of Vermont–Burlington, 2003.

"Ezra Butler Eddy." Wikipedia, the free encyclopedia. http://en.wikipedia.org/wiki/Ezra_Butler_Eddy.

Flowers, John. "Residents bid farewell to Fred Jackman." *Addison Independent*, December 31, 2008.

Hanson, Kevin, Audrey Dike and Ruth Lathrop. "Bristol Houses." Interview. July 15, 1999. Bristol Historical Society, no accession number, audiocassette.

Heffernan, Gerald. "The Evolution and Demise of Drake & Smith Company of Bristol." Unpublished paper prepared for the Bristol Historical Society, n.d.

Heffernan, Gerald, Leslie Leggett and Libby Steadman. Interview. 2006. "VanRaalte workers." Bristol Historical Society, accession number 2006.001.001, audiocassette.

Ives, Mike. "Bristol Zoning Board Rejects Gravel Pit Proposal." *Seven Days*, September 26, 2008.

Kilbourn, Alan. Personal interview by Kerry K. Skiffington, December 12, 2008.

Lathrop, George. Interview. 2001. Bristol Historical Society, accession number 2001.003.017 (side 2), audiocassette.

Lathrop, Gertrude Hewitt. Interview. 2007. Bristol Historical Society, accession number 2007.036.001, audiocassette.

Levarn, Gussie, and Rosie Levarn. Interview. 1994. "Voices from Vermont." Vermont Folklife Center, accession number TC1994.0080.

Levarn, Gussie. "Gussie Levarn Reflects." Interview. 2005. Bristol Historical Society, accession number 2005.015.001, audiocassette.

———. "Voices from Vermont." Interview. 1994. Vermont Folklife Center, accession number TC1994.0081.

Lewis, Martin, and Gerald Heffernan. "Little Ireland." Interview. June 19, 2003. Bristol Historical Society, no accession number, audiocassette.

Martin, Nellie. Interview. 2001. Bristol Historical Society, accession number 2001.003.018 (side 2), audiocassette.

McKinnon, Sam. "Survey." Interview. 1998. Vermont Folklife Center, accession number TC1998.0017.

Munsill, Honorable Harvey, Esq. *The Early History of Bristol, Vermont, Formerly Known as Pocock.* Bristol, VT: Bristol Historical Society, circa 1870.

Outlook Club of Bristol. *History of Bristol, Vermont (1762–1940).* First Edition. Bristol, VT: Bristol Historical Society, 1940.

———. *History of Bristol, Vermont (1762–1980).* Third Edition. Bristol, VT: Bristol Historical Society, 1980.

Peake, Peveril. Interview. 2001. Bristol Historical Society, accession number 2001.003.022, audiocassette.

———. "Peake Family Collection." Unpublished manuscript, courtesy of the Bristol Historical Society, n.d.

Pecor, Josie. Interview. 2001. Bristol Historical Society, accession number 2001.003.020, audiocassette.

Raymond, Wiser and associated Cleve and Anita Raymond Progenitors. http://freepages.genealogy.rootsweb.ancestry.com/~raymondfamily?Vermont/Bristol Village 1871.

Selden, Jack. Interview. 2001. Bristol Historical Society, accession number 2001.7.20, audiocassette.

Skiffington, Kerry K. "Noblesse Oblige: A Strategy of Local Boundary Making." *Ethnology* (July 1991): 265–77.

Smith, H.P., ed. "History of the Town of Bristol." Chap. 18 in *History of Addison County, Vermont.* Syracuse, NY: D. Mason & Co. Publishers, 1886. http://www.middlebury.edu/academics/lis/lib/guides_and_tutorials/subject_guides/collection_guide-vermont/internet_resources/history_addison_county/chap18_hac.htm.

Swift, Samuel. "Diseases, Mortality." Chap. 17 in *History of the Town of Middlebury.* Middlebury, VT: Middlebury Historical Society, 1859.

Thomson, Zadock. "Diseases of Vermont." Sec. 8 in *History of Vermont.* Montpelier, VT, 1842.

Tyler, George, and George Smith. "Remembering Bristol." Interview. 2007. Bristol Historical Society, accession number 2007.034.001, audiocassette.

Tyler, George, George Smith and Gerald Heffernan. Interview by Mount Abraham Union High School students. 2003. Bristol Historical Society, accession number 2003.034.001, audiocassette.

Wallace, W. Stewart. *Encyclopedia of Canada.* Toronto, Ontario: University Associates of Canada, 1948. http://faculty.marianopolis.edu/c.belanger/QuebecHistory/encyclopedia/EzraButlerEddy.htm.

Weston, Ken. "History of Bristol Band." Interview. 2007. Bristol Historical Society, accession number 2007.022.001, audiocassette.

Visit us at
www.historypress.net